PROJECT 2
URBAN LEGE

BY
MARK BARBER

www.project2067.com

© Copyright 2005 Mark Barber.

All rights reserved. No part of this publication may be reproduced, stored in a retrieval system, or transmitted, in any form or by any means, electronic, mechanical, photocopying, recording, or otherwise, without the written prior permission of the author.

Printed in Victoria, BC, Canada

Note for Librarians: a cataloguing record for this book that includes Dewey Decimal Classification and US Library of Congress numbers is available from the Library and Archives of Canada. The complete cataloguing record can be obtained from their online database at:
www.collectionscanada.ca/amicus/index-e.html
ISBN 1-4120-4546-0

TRAFFORD

This book was published on-demand in cooperation with Trafford Publishing. On-demand publishing is a unique process and service of making a book available for retail sale to the public taking advantage of on-demand manufacturing and Internet marketing. On-demand publishing includes promotions, retail sales, manufacturing, order fulfilment, accounting and collecting royalties on behalf of the author.

Offices in Canada, USA, UK, Ireland, and Spain
book sales for North America and international:
Trafford Publishing, 6E-2333 Government St.
Victoria, BC V8T 4P4 CANADA
phone 250 383 6864   toll-free 1 888 232 4444
fax 250 383 6804   email to orders@trafford.com

book sales in Europe:
Trafford Publishing (UK) Ltd., Enterprise House, Wistaston Road Business Centre
Crewe, Cheshire CW2 7RP UNITED KINGDOM
phone 01270 251 396   local rate 0845 230 9601
facsimile 01270 254 983   orders.uk@trafford.com

order online at:
www.trafford.com/robots/04-2354.html

Acknowledgements…

This project has taken 4 years to complete, and would not have been possible without the help, support and patience from the following people:

Joanna, Mum (for the tedious task of proof-reading my work), Dad, Jayne, Whizz, Nan, Prof. Jan Harold Brunvand, Pep, Patrick Arnick (broodjeaap.nl), Sofia Knapp (Valmyndigheten), Maud Gehrman, NG Dave, Barbara & David P.Mikkelson (Snopes.com), the AFU and Urban Legends Archive, Sarah Newcombe (Trafford Publishing), and to the rest of my friends and family – you know who you are!

Project 2067 is dedicated to…

Holly (my little princess)

CONTENTS...

INTRODUCTION...PAGE 5

CLASSIC HORROR...PAGE 9

JUST FOR LAUGHS..PAGE 27

CRIME..PAGE 49

ANIMALS & PESTS...PAGE 71

HORROR..PAGE 95

TRAINS, PLANES, & AUTOMOBILES...............PAGE 119

FOOD & DRINK...PAGE 149

AROUND THE WORLD......................................PAGE 171

NETLORE...PAGE 197

9\11...PAGE 221

PARODIES...PAGE 253

FINAL REPORT..PAGE 265

QUICK GUIDE STATUS SUMMARY...................PAGE 278

INTRODUCTION

Project 2067: Introduction

New York, don't you just love it? Colder than an Eskimo's arse in the winter, hotter than the flames of hell in the summer. Right now it is the latter, and the heat is unbearable. I am sitting in my shoebox of an office on the 47th floor of a skyscraper on 53rd Street, Manhattan. The air-conditioning has packed up yet again, and the only thing to keep me cool is a cheap fan that imitates the sound of a mosquito! That with the constant sounds of car horns and the distant whaling of police sirens, I am finding it impossible to concentrate with the job in hand. But concentrate I must do, because this is my big break, the chance I have been waiting for, and some people feel I shouldn't be here!

By now you must be wondering what Project 2067 is, I am coming to that, but first I must introduce myself. My name is Jarvis Redman and I am an investigative journalist working for the Daily National newspaper back in London, England. I started working for the Daily National straight from leaving school, and over the last 5 years I have crawled my way up through the ranks kissing many butts along the way. But now I have my chance, Project 2067 can make or break my career. It is up to me! It is a mammoth task, as I look out over the scrawling landscape of towering skyscrapers piercing the sky, and the hustle and bustle of the streets simmering below. London, home, feels further away than ever from this urban jungle. I never thought I could feel so alone in a place that has so many people!

Yeah, Yeah! Pass the bucket – I know! You haven't come here to hear some sob story, so without further delay, let's "cut to the chase!" as they say in the Big Apple. Project 2067 is the brainchild of the Daily National's editor Max Allen, and is the code name for an assignment he has sent me on. The assignment is to investigate the subject of 'Urban Legends'. I know investigating 'Urban Legends' is hardly like finding the Holy Grail, or discovering the meaning of life, but there is a reason for all the secrecy and my job depends on it.

Angus Brute is a media tycoon and owns over half of the newspapers back home. Not only does he own most of the newspapers, he also runs the digital and cable TV networks, has a stake in all the major football clubs (even Leicester!), and controls the two biggest commercial radio stations in the country. To put it bluntly, Angus Brute is the big shark in these waters, and he considers the Daily National as a small fish way out of its depth. Angus is a ruthless man with a vision, and plans to hold a monopoly on the whole media spectrum, crushing anyone in his way. So you see, he really has us caught by our 'short and curlies' and we are fighting for the Daily Nationals very existence.

PROJECT 2067

With Project 2067 we are hoping to peel away the many layers of Urban Legends to hopefully uncover their interesting, sometimes sinister, and sometimes political underbelly. By uncovering these truths it may supply us with the big exclusive we are looking for to bring back our readers, and hopefully keep them! Angus already has an inkling that we are up to something, and is using all his powers of intimidation to find out what. This is why the story is shrouded in secrecy. If Angus gets the slightest whiff of Project 2067, he could stop it in its tracks and claim the exclusive to himself, sealing the fate of the Daily National.

Before carrying on, I must briefly explain to you what 'Urban Legends' are. Urban Legends (UL's) are tales of modern folklore that can be passed on through traditional methods such as 'word of mouth', or by modern methods such as E-Mail, faxes, and the Internet. Variations of the same UL can be heard in many different countries spontaneously spreading like a virus and often mutating to the environment they are told in, with details being localised by the storyteller. UL's often play on the fears, beliefs, and anxieties of a particular period or moment in time, and over the years the legends adjust to reflect the themes of the new modern era. For example, The *Vanishing Hitchhiker* (HR4704) is a classic and one of the oldest ULs. In the story, the mode of transport has changed over the years to adapt with the times. The transport has changed from horseback and 'Horse and Chariot' in the early legends, then to the 'Horse and wagon', and eventually to the modern versions with a car.

Because the legends often reflect the 'sign of the times', they often contain morals or lessons that are embedded within the tale. It may be possible to use the influence of UL's to manipulate and to use as a propaganda tool for political motives, or for more sinister gains. This is an area that I hope to tap into and uncover some truths!

The answers to the following questions interest UL investigators the most:

1. How and where did the legend originate from?
2. How has the legend spread?

The answers to these questions are not as easy as you may think, as the legends are normally totally believed to be true by the teller. The teller will probably tell you that he/she had heard the story from someone they know (i.e. friend or relative), and if you asked the friend/relative about the story, they would probably tell you it has actually happened to someone *they* know. The same pattern will repeat itself again and again, leading to a dead end at every turn and

INTRODUCTION

the investigator around the bend! It is this complicated set of events that led the author Rodney Dale coining the term (FOAF), which simply means "A Friend Of A Friend".

Tracing the origins of the legends can also be a frustrating business because the legends have a habit of mutating over the years, and so may have originally reflected a totally different set of events to which they do now. Of course, not all UL's are an impressive work of fiction, some are true and others contain an element of truth. Sometimes the borders between fiction and reality are blurred so much it is impossible to tell one from the other. As they say (don't ask me who), the truth can be stranger than fiction.

UL's can cover every subject you can imagine, and like jokes, seem to arrive on the scene immediately after an important event has happened. At present, UL's are thriving with the use of modern technology. The spread of the legends, which used to be very reliant on the word of mouth process, are spread rapidly by faxes, E-Mail and the Internet. This gives the legends an instant global audience. The flip side of the coin is that the new technology is very vulnerable to hoaxes. UL's in particular have thrived on the fear of computer viruses, spreading worldwide panic over something that is nothing more than a hoax.

Ok! Now I have brought you up to speed, it's time to tell you where you fit in to all this. If you thought this was going to be a nice bedtime story you could read while sipping your hot cocoa in bed, you are in for a shock! Wake up and smell the coffee (or should I say cocoa?). You are now part of this investigation, and I need all the help I can get. So, please sharpen your mind and be prepared to think (some of you may have to look up that last word in the dictionary!), and read on.

This is how it will work. The Urban Legends will be split up into different categories, and each UL (Urban Legend) will have at least one version to the story. At the top of each UL, will be the following headings:

NAME: *The name of the UL*

CODE: *The reference that this particular UL is filed under*

ORIGIN: *Where the UL originated from and the period of time*

STATUS: *If the UL is believed to be true or false, or whether it is undecided*

The Code can be used to access a particular UL on the Project 2067 website that I have set up. On the website you will be able to access greater information on selected ULs. Maybe different versions of the story, different endings, and different beliefs into the origin of the UL. Not only will you be able to send in your own findings, arguments and opinions, you will also be able to view what other readers have sent in as well.

Do you see the big picture now? I need you to help me research these UL's; do you know a different version, and where and when did you first hear it? But most importantly I would also like to hear any arguments on the origins and theories behind the UL's. Do you know if they are true or false, and if they are false why were they started and how? With your help, I will uncover the shroud of mystery that surrounds the purpose and origins of these legends. After all, to fully understand, you have to go to the heart of the matter and find out what makes it 'tick'.

Now, I know what you are thinking. Why should you bother to help out a stressed out, coffee breathed chump like me. Well, first of all I would like to think that you have a mutual interest in the subject. If you had no knowledge of UL's beforehand, I am sure you are as intrigued into the subject as I was when I first came across them. Secondly, if you have just come along for the ride, stick around! I will take you to some interesting and far out places en-route. Anyway, what else are you going to do? It's not like there is anything on TV worth watching! Lets go 'smoke' some Urban Legends!

CLASSIC HORROR...

INTRODUCTION...PAGE 10

BACKSEAT HITCHHIKER...PAGE 11

THE HOOK...PAGE 14

KNOCK, KNOCK, KNOCK...PAGE 16

THE VANISHING HITCHHIKER.................................PAGE 18

BLOODY MARY..PAGE 20

THE ROOMMATE'S DEATH...PAGE 23

LIGHTS OUT..PAGE 25

Monday, 15th August
13.00hrs: The office

CATEGORY: CLASSIC HORROR

I consider this category the 'bread and butter' of UL's. These tales offer horror in its most simplistic and purest form that gets delivered straight to the heart like an adrenalin rush. They form the backbone to most modern horror stories, with the modern slasher/horror films heavily dependent and influenced by UL's. These tales survive the hands of time because of one basic reason; they make 'good story telling'. A Cub Scout Campfire would be meaningless without at least one of these UL's been told while heating marshmallows over the open flames! Also, after the campfire in the tent with your friends, while huddled into your sleeping bag, you would be telling me a 'porky pie' if you claim that you have never laid awake once the darkness of night has settled in, replaying the stories like an old 'B' Movie in your mind. Dark shadows slipping over the tent, the 'hoot' of an owl followed by scuffling noises from the nearby wood. Are those footsteps you can hear? Is that a hook you can make out from the shadows crawling across the canopy?

After reading the 'Bloody Mary' story I dare you (no, no – I *double* dare you) to repeat the name 5 times while looking in a mirror. You know it isn't real, but bogeymen *do* exist, and are lurking somewhere in the back of your mind. UL's tap into this basic fear and exploit it, and that is what makes them so effective.

While you are studying the following cases, I am going to go down to the diner on the corner of East 58th Street to get my regular fix of caffeine. It has been two hours since I last had a coffee, something that is unheard of in the Big Apple! So without further delay, lets move on. Best not be late, for you have a date with the bogeyman…

CLASSIC HORROR

NAME: **Backseat Hitchhiker**
CODE: **HR4701**
ORIGIN: **1967, USA**
STATUS: **False**

Backseat Hitchhiker: Example A

As a girl is driving back home along a dark country lane after a night out with the girls in Bracknell, Berkshire (England), she comes across a dog lying in the middle of the road. Being a fond animal lover, she immediately stops and dashes over to the dog to see if it is dead or just injured. After approaching the dog, the headlights of a car appear in the distance behind her. After a quick examination of the dog she realises it is dead and moves the body to the side of the road.

By now the approaching car is near, so she rushes back to her car and pulls away swiftly. As soon as she does this, the car behind accelerates right up behind her. The girl looks in her rear view mirror to see the man driving making hand gestures of some kind at her. He then starts beeping his horn and continuously flashing his lights. By now the girl is petrified and accelerates even more to try and shake off the nutter. The pursuer keeps up. Still flashing his lights and beeping his horn.

This pursuit carries on for another couple of miles before the girl finally reaches home, and speedily pulls up onto her drive. She immediately rushes into her house; double locks the door and rushes to the window. The man who had pursued her was now running up her drive. He reaches her car just as another man is climbing out from the back seat. The pursuer grapples the man to the floor and calls for the girl to call the police. The police promptly arrive and arrest the man who had climbed out from the backseat of her car.

Later, the man in the pursuing car told the police that he had spotted a man climb into the backseat of the girl's car when she had been attending to the dead dog. He had followed her frantically trying to catch her attention. Every time he saw the mans head bob up from the backseat, he beeped his horn and flashed his lights to put him off. The man from the backseat has now been taken back to the jail he escaped from, serving a sentence for murder.

PROJECT 2067

Backseat Hitchhiker: Example B

It was a dark and foggy night. This girl was having trouble staying awake and the road was slick. Her anxiety level was not helped by the fact that she was running low on petrol and didn't know where the next town was. Finally, just as she thought she would have to pull over and sleep till morning on the side of the road, she saw a run down petrol station and pulled in. The petrol attendant approached the car but seemed distracted when she asked him to fill her car up. As the attendant was filling the car with petrol he kept looking over at the girl in a way that gave her the creeps and made her feel increasingly vulnerable. After the attendant had finished, the girl handed over all money she had, which happened to be the exact money for payment. The attendant told her it was not enough and she would have to step into his office. The girl felt incredibly scared and worried as she followed him into the small office, as she knew that the amount she had given him was correct. As soon as she stepped into the office the attendant slammed the door shut behind her, and she felt like she was going to scream. The attendant hurriedly explained that he had to drag her away from the vehicle as he had observed a man crouching down in her back seat, and didn't want the man to realise that he had been spotted.

The attendant called the police who promptly arrived and arrested the man. The girl later found out that the man was a wanted serial killer, and had stowed away in her car waiting for the right moment to pounce.

Summary

I first heard 'Example A' when I was very young, and this UL has been doing the rounds in one format or another for many years. It is believed that the legend first entered the scene in 1967, becoming one of the most popular horror stories of that period. Although versions do vary, the core elements of this UL remain the same; the intended victim is always female and always misreads the intentions of the male rescuer. The rescuer is always astute, either luring the female away from danger, or beeping his horn and flashing his lights every time the madman pops up from the backseat, forcing him back into hiding. The stranger in the backseat is always male, and either a lone madman/serial killer, or part of a gang initiation. His intentions are rarely clearly defined, and you are left to draw your own conclusions.

Final Thoughts

Although it is popular belief that there are grains of truth in this UL, I believe that it was originally told as a warning to lone females to be vigilant when travelling at night. It is also a story of stereotyping, with the lone female always jumping to the wrong conclusion about the rescuer's intentions. Not realising the real danger was much closer than she thought.

PROJECT 2067

NAME: The Hook
CODE: HR4702
ORIGIN: At least since the 1950's USA
STATUS: Undecided

The Hook

As a young teenage couple are driving along to a remote lover's lane, a news flash interrupts the song on the radio announcing that a serial killer has just escaped from the local prison, and is considered extremely dangerous. The announcer warns for people to stay in their houses and not to go out unless it is necessary. He also says the killer can easily be recognised as he has a hook in place of a hand. The young girl looks worriedly at her boyfriend and tells him she is scared and wants to go home. He calmly tells her there is nothing to be worried about, and besides, he is there to protect her! The girl calms down and they proceed to the lover's lane.

Just after they start getting *jiggy* with it, the girl hears a rustling noise from the nearby woods and gets frantically scared. She pleads with her boyfriend to take her home, but he is very reluctant and an argument ensues. The girl is so frantic that the boyfriend eventually gives in. The boyfriend turns the ignition key, and roars away down the lane in utter frustration.

After a journey in sulky silence, the young couple arrive at the girl's house. The boyfriend (even though mad with her, hasn't forgotten his manners) gets out of the car and walks around the other side to open her door. He stops dead, turns as white as a ghost and faints. The girlfriend hurriedly gets out of the car to tend to him. As she shuts the car doors behind her, she hears a 'clank' and turns around. There, swinging backwards and forwards is a bloody hook dangling on the door handle.

Summary

'The Hook' needs no introduction! If you have never heard this story, then I welcome you to our planet, and I am sure you come in peace! This UL has been kicking around the campfires since at least the 1950's, although it's origins are unclear. This story is particularly scary, as it brings up the scenario of 'What if'. The teenage couple obviously escape with their lives at the last moment, and it is a chain of events that lead to their lucky escape. If the young girl had let her boyfriend get his own way and decided to stay, then they would not have escaped. This is also true if the boyfriend hadn't have been so annoyed and stepped on the accelerator, roaring off down the lane. This very action leads to the climax of the story, with the bloody hook left dangling on the door handle. This image is a realisation of what could have been!

Final Thoughts

This UL may have been based on events that actually happened. The story probably has been altered to give a more dramatic and scary effect, but the basic outline may have been based on true-life experiences. It is reported that Lover Lane murders did occur in the 1940's, but none as far as I know, by a man with a hook for a hand.

I think that this UL gives a good dose of the 1950's moral standards. This period saw the explosion of 'Rock 'n' Roll', and in it's wake, teenage rebellion. This was the first time that a true 'Generation Gap' was created, and parents treated Rock and Roll as the new evil (even worse than Eminem!). Teenage girls found a new confidence, and started to rebel against their parent's old-fashioned views. They started going out with boys more freely, and this was seen as a threat by the parents. That is why I believe UL's like this one, were made up to warn teenage girls not to let their morals slip. After all, if the girl in this story succumbed to her boyfriend's wishes, she would have paid with her life, and that is a pretty raw deal!

So enough with the history lesson, next week will be Algebra – oh no!

PROJECT 2067

NAME: Knock, Knock, Knock
CODE: HR4703
ORIGIN: Descendant from 'The Hook'
STATUS: False

Knock, Knock, Knock: Example 1

A teenage couple are driving back home late one night along a lane through woodland, when the car runs out of petrol. The boyfriend pulls over into a lay-by and explains to the girlfriend that there is a petrol station only a couple of miles up the road, and if he runs he will be back in no time. The girlfriend, unconvinced, pleads him not to leave her alone. The boyfriend tells her that if she is scared, she can hide under the blanket on the backseat. When he returns, he will knock on the roof three times. Under no circumstances is she to open the door if she hears any less or more than three knocks. The girlfriend agrees, and after her boyfriend leaves the car she climbs into the backseat.

Twenty minutes later she hears a knock on the roof. Then another one, and then a third. She is just about to get up when she hears another knock. Now petrified, she sinks back into the backseat pulling the blanket tight over her. Further knocks on the roof follow and the girl panics. She quickly climbs over into the drivers seat, turns the ignition on and goes to accelerate away. The car surges forward a couple of meters and then conks out. The girlfriend decides her only escape will be to make a run for it. She opens the door and glances back before making a dash for it, but what she sees makes her freeze in her tracks. There, hanging from a branch with a noose around his neck, is her boyfriend. He had been bound above the car, and the tapping noises on the roof of the car was caused by her boyfriend trying to keep his balance, just managing to reach the roof while standing on tiptoes. She had killed her boyfriend!

Knock, Knock, Knock: Example 2

The first part of this version is exactly the same as Example 1, so we will pick up the story after the boyfriend has left the car to run down to the petrol station. His girlfriend has climbed into the backseat and pulled the blanket over her, waiting for the three knocks to signal his return:

16

CLASSIC HORROR

Over half-an-hour passes and the girlfriend is feeling increasingly worried. When all of a sudden she hears the knock on the roof, quickly followed by a second and then a third. She feels relieved that her boyfriend has returned, but before she has time to get up, she hears another two thuds on the roof. Remembering what her boyfriend told her about the three knocks, she is now petrified and pulls the blanket even further over her head.

After a couple of hours she drifts off to sleep, only to wake startled by flashlights shining through the windows, and the wailing of police sirens. She hears a police officer speaking through a megaphone ordering her out of the vehicle. He tells her to approach the police car rapidly and not to look back. The girl climbs out of the car and starts to run to where the officer is standing, but of course the temptation is too much and she glances back over her shoulder. There, on the roof of her car, stands a grinning man with fierce wild eyes. At first she didn't notice what he was holding, but she soon realised that he was holding her boyfriend's severed head by the hair.

Summary

Knock, Knock, Knock is also known as 'The Boyfriends Death', and is strongly related to the 'Hook'. In fact, some alternative endings to *Example 2* have the maniac standing on the roof of her car with a Hook for a hand, holding her boyfriends severed head in the other hand. I believe that this UL has branched off from the original 'Hook' legend, and over the years has gained it's own identity. The main difference between the two UL's, is that in the 'Hook' it was a close shave. If they had delayed their exit slightly, then the lovers would have been 'Brown Bread'. Instead, they just got away in the knick of time, and the surprise at the end was a realisation of this fact. In 'Knock, Knock, Knock' they are not so lucky. The girlfriend loses her boyfriend, and the boyfriend loses his head! *Example 1* gives a double turn of the knife, not only does the girl realise her boyfriend is dead, but she has accidentally sealed his fate. As UL's go, not the happiest of endings!

Final Thoughts

There are so many different versions of this story, making it one of the most versatile UL's I have known. In recent years this legend has become as popular, if not more so, than the original source (The Hook).

PROJECT 2067

```
NAME:     The Vanishing Hitchhiker
CODE:     HR4704
ORIGIN:   Unknown
STATUS:   Undecided
```

The Vanishing Hitchhiker

A young doctor was driving back home from an evening out one Saturday night, when he had to stop for traffic lights at a busy junction. As he looked over to the side of the road, he was surprised to see a very pretty young girl, dressed in a lovely evening gown, beckoning him for a lift. As he had his golf bag leaning on his front seat, the doctor motioned for the girl to climb in the backseat, which she did. Still astounded by her beauty, the doctor asked her "What on earth are you doing walking around here at this time of night?"

The young girl simply replied "It's a long story, can you please take me home?"

The doctor said that he would and asked her where she lived. The address was a long way out of his way, but he agreed to take her home. The journey did not take as long as he had expected, and they had spent most of the journey in silence. When the doctor arrived at the address she had given him, he turned around to tell her they had arrived; but she had vanished!

The doctor, now feeling confused and in a state of disbelief, knocked on the door of the house where the girl had told him she had lived. A frail old man opened the door and the doctor tried to explain. "I don't quite know how to tell you this; I gave a young girl a lift and she told me she lived at this address. When I arrived…"

The old man raised his hand up to signal the doctor to stop talking, and spoke to him in a very direct but weary voice. "The young girl was my daughter, she was killed in a car accident on her way back home after her prom night. This happened 7 years ago today, and every year I meet a different gentleman and have this same conversation as I am having with you."

Summary

The origins of this UL are unknown, but this version goes back to at least the turn of the last century. The origins can be traced back a lot further than that though, and there is even a version in the most famous book of all time (No, no, I am not talking about a Harry Potter book!), I am talking about the Bible. You don't believe me? Well if you reminisce back to your glorious days of Sunday school, you may remember (or not!) the story of the Ethiopian who picks up the Apostle Philip in his chariot. Who baptises the Ethiopian and then promptly disappears! New Testament (Acts 8:26-39). Not many UL's can stake a claim to being in the Bible!

The more modern version has still been disappearing in backseats for centuries, believed to be firmly rooted in Middle Aged European folklore. Of course, they didn't have cars in those days, and the girl would disappear on horseback. As the centuries rolled on, the form of transport changed to the horse and wagon, and eventually to the car, as we know it today.

Final Thoughts

So what makes this UL so special that it has remained a popular story throughout the centuries? I think the main reason is that if you strip this UL down to the bone, you are left with a classic ghost story. The fact that the 'ghost' appears to be so realistic and actually has a conversion with the driver, makes this UL even more disturbing. I mean this isn't a Scooby Doo ghost, which ends up being the old professor with a sheet over his head. This is more like a ragged looking Bruce Willis with "I see dead people" still ringing in his ear!

If you peel away the surface of this legend, it appears that the dead girl is lost between worlds (no, I don't know what I am talking about!) and the scenario of the girl's fatal journey home that Saturday night years before, being replayed over and over again like a scratched CD, with her final thought of getting home safely still haunting her. Well I hope you will all sleep soundly tonight; I know I won't!

PROJECT 2067

NAME: Bloody Mary
CODE: HR4705
ORIGIN: Unknown
STATUS: False

Bloody Mary

A group of girls are having a sleepover, and sometime during the night they decide to take it in turns to tell each other ghost stories. By the time the story telling reaches Anne's turn, all the girls are already feeling freaked out. After thinking hard, Anne decides to tell a story that her Aunty used to tell her. The name of the story is 'Bloody Mary' and goes something like this:

Over one hundred years ago, a woman by the name of 'Mary Worth' was lynched from her family home by an angry mob accusing her of witchcraft. She was tortured and then burned at the stake witnessed by the whole village. As the burning flames engulfed her, she screamed out a curse damning the whole village.

It is said that the vengeful spirit of Mary Worth can be summoned by looking directly into a mirror after it is dark and with no lights on. After repeating 'Bloody Mary' five times, her face will appear in the mirror and…well, no one knows!

After Anne has told her story, the girls are shocked into silence. After a short period they start giggling nervously and dare each other to go into the bathroom, turn out the lights, look into the mirror and repeat 'Bloody Mary' five times. Anne takes up the challenge and tells the girls that it was just a story and that she doesn't believe in Mary Worth anyway.

Anne enters the bathroom, and the girls hear her repeat 'Bloody Mary' five times. After the fifth time there is deadly silence, and the girls start knocking on the bathroom door asking if Anne was all right. After a few minutes the door slowly opens and Anne appears in the doorway. She is visibly shaking and has gone as white as a ghost. She is clenching her fists so hard that she has drawn blood in the palms of her hand.

Anne could never tell the girls what actually happened in that bathroom, and has never been able to talk about it since!

Summary

A story to spice up any sleepover, don't you agree? An absolute classic horror tale that has all the ingredients for a UL, with garnish sprinkled on top. The tale actually incorporates a story within a story, making it seem very real, and very disturbing. The main story centres around a sleepover with a bunch of girls. I am sure that almost everyone reading this (boys and girls) has been involved in a sleepover of some kind, and can relate to the story. I mean, who hasn't told scary stories, trying to spook each other once the lights have gone out?

The story that Anne told was different though, like playing with a Ouija board, innocent fun can turn dangerous. As the old saying goes *'if you play with matches, you will get burnt!'* So why did Anne tempt fate by going in the bathroom and summoning the ghost of Mary Worth? I think we all know that answer; it's the thrill of the dare, the excitement of facing the unknown.

The name of the spirit that is summoned varies from version to version; the following are the most popular:

Bloody Mary	Mary Worth	Hell Mary	Mary Worthington
Mary Whales	Mary Johnson	Mary Lou	Mary Jane
Kathy	Sally	Agnes	Bloody Bones
Svarte Madame	La Llorna	The Devil	

The amount of times that the name is chanted into the mirror also varies from version to version. One variant is that you begin by chanting the name in a whisper, after each chant you raise your voice gradually. After the 13th chant Mary Worth appears in the mirror and slashes your face. Normally the chant is "Bloody Mary", but also can be "I believe in Mary Worth" or "Kathy, come out!"

Final Thoughts

The origins of this UL cannot be easily traced, although throughout the history of mythology mirrors have often been used as a gateway to other dimensions. In the past, mirrors have been covered up after there has been a death in the house. This is so the spirit of the deceased cannot glimpse at it's self in a mirror, damning the spirit to haunt our world forever.

Another interesting link to this UL is that in the old days young girls used to carry out a similar ritual. After reciting a rhyme, an unmarried girl would glimpse into a mirror to see the image of her future husband.

Another version of 'Bloody Mary' has the spirit of Mary Worth walking along roadsides looking for her children that were murdered. If a car picks her up, she disappears before reaching her destination. This version has very strong similarities to 'The Vanishing Hitchhiker' and is probably linked in some way.

CLASSIC HORROR

NAME: The Roommate's Death
CODE: HR4706
ORIGIN: 1950's USA
STATUS: False

The Roommate's Death: Version 1

A girl at college returned to her Dorm late one night to collect her books and some stuff, before returning to her boyfriends Dorm to stay the night. When she entered the room it was dark, but she didn't want to turn the lights on knowing that her roommate was sleeping. She stumbled around in the dark, gathering her books, clothes and her toothbrush, before leaving quietly.

The next day she returned to the room, only to find it surrounded by police. An Officer asked her if she was living there, with which she replied "yes". He also asked her if she had returned back to the dorm last night, with which she also replied "Yes, but only for a few minutes." The officer then told her that her roommate had been murdered, and asked the girl to step into the room.

As the girl walked into bedroom, she froze with fright. On the wall, written in blood, was the following message 'AREN'T YOU GLAD YOU DIDN'T TURN ON THE LIGHT?'

The Roommate's Death: Version 2

Two Roommates in college were taking the same class together, and were taking an exam the next day's afternoon. Although being reminded of the importance of the exam by their teacher, Sarah had arranged to go out on a hot date with the college hunk, and had no intention of revising. Stacy on the other hand was a perfect student, and had organised all her notes ready for a night of heavy revising.

That evening, Sarah spent hours putting on her make-up while Stacy had already settled down with her books. The girls were very close and Stacy tried her hardest to persuade Sarah to stay in and study, worried she would fail the course. Sarah had none of it, her excuse being she would revise for the exam in the morning.

After returning from her hot date, Sarah returned to the dorm about 2am. As she entered her room, Sarah heard a muffled noise coming from Stacy's bed. She presumed Stacy was tossing and turning in her sleep, and crept past her bed without turning on the light, so not to wake her.

Sarah woke up late the next morning and was surprised to see Stacy still lying in bed. As Sarah went over to wake Stacy, she was horrified to see the covers of the bed were soaked with blood. Sarah rushed over to the bed and pulled Stacy over so she was facing upwards, Stacy had been stabbed to death. Sarah stumbled backwards deeply shocked and fell to the floor. As she looked up, she saw the following message scrawled across the wall in blood *'Aren't you glad you didn't turn on the light?'*

Summary

These versions are sometimes named 'Aren't you glad you didn't turn on the light?' and are just two of many variations. The common factor in all the versions is that the murder is taking place right under the nose of the unsuspecting roommate, and the killer scrawling the message in blood on the wall rubs in this fact. If the girl had turned on the lights, she would have been the next victim for sure.

Final Thoughts

This is another UL from the 1950's, and again a popular UL amongst the colleges in the USA. As with most other teenage horrors, a moral message is embedded within the story. A simple warning that danger can be lurking around any corner, and it pays to be careful. In other words, another cautionary UL whipped up by extremely paranoid parents!

CLASSIC HORROR

```
NAME:      Lights Out
CODE:      HR4707
ORIGIN:    Early 1980's:  USA
STATUS:    False
```

Lights Out: Version 1; 1998

Police Departments across the USA are issuing the following warning to motorists when driving at night: If you see an on-coming car without its headlights on, *do not* flash your headlights at the car under any circumstance. This may be part of a known initiation game carried out by new gang members. If you flash at the car, you will become their new target. They will turn around and give chase to you, and as part of the initiation they will try and gun you down.

This is becoming a very serious matter, and we would like you to warn your friends and family. Please take heed!

Lights Out: Version 2; August 1993

Police Departments across the nation are being warned that on September 25th and 26th will be the 'blood' initiation weekend. All the new bloods (new gang members) will drive around on the Saturday and Sunday nights with their headlights off. In order to be accepted into the gang, they have to shoot and kill all the individuals in the first car that makes a courtesy flash to warn them that their lights are off.

Summary

This UL has had three main outbreaks, in the early 1980's, August 1993 and in 1997. The first main outbreak in the early 1980's was originated in California, and the gang involved were the 'Hells Angels'. The UL spread slowly but with conviction. By 1984 the story had spread to Eugene, Oregon (USA) and the gangs involved were now supposed to be black and Hispanic LA street gangs targeting white people.

The second outbreak was in August 1993, and with the use of faxes and E-mails it spread rapidly. This time it was a warning about the 'blood' initiation weekend, which was supposed to happen on the 25th and 26th of September (1993). Of course, the weekend came and went without incident.

The 'Lights Out' UL disappeared for a few years before resurfacing in 1998, bigger and bolder than ever. The new outbreak sent the US into a frenzy, with government and city departments sending out official warnings of the danger. The warnings were quickly withdrawn, but the damage had already been done.

Final Thoughts

The 'Lights Out' legend is false, although a believed copycat incident did occur. In 1993 a man named David Vargyas (Ohio, US) was shot and injured while being a passenger in a car. The driver had flashed his lights as a warning to a car travelling in the opposite direction without its headlights on. The car gave chase and three shots were fired injuring Mr Vargyas.

Another incident occurred in 1992, when Kelly Freed (California, US) was shot dead while being a passenger in a car. The driver had made a hand signal to some youths travelling the opposite way without their headlights on. The hand gesture was supposed to be signal for them to turn their lights on, but it was perceived as a rude gesture, and the kids gave chase and shot into the car.

Was this UL started as a hypothetical warning about the increasing problem of gang initiation activities? Or like certain violent films, does it just exploit and incite this kind of mindless violence? Your call!

JUST FOR LAUGHS...

INTRODUCTION..PAGE 28

FART IN THE DARK..PAGE 29

THE COLLEGE LETTER.....................................PAGE 31

THE PARISIAN BELLBOY..................................PAGE 33

STAND OFF AT SEA...PAGE 35

THE CAT FLAP..PAGE 36

THE BISCUIT BULLET......................................PAGE 38

THE BRICKLAYER...PAGE 40

THE NAKED SKIER...PAGE 42

TAKE THE TUBE...PAGE 44

THE UNZIPPED FLY..PAGE 46

PROJECT 2067

Monday, 15th August
14.30hrs: Dusty's Diner, East 58th St.

CATEGORY: JUST FOR LAUGHS

All I wanted was a cup of coffee, white with no sugar; is that really too much to ask for? Apparently, yes! The girl in the coffee shop asked me what I wanted, to which I replied "A cup of coffee please".

She then replied, "What kind do you want? We have Cappuccino, Caffe Latte, Caffe Mocha, Espresso, Espresso choc, Espresso Macchiato, Americano, iced coffee, decaf, and regular small, medium or large?"

My brain now scrambled and in the need for caffeine, I asked for a regular large. Amongst the mind boggling list she spilled out to me was the word decaf'. What is the point of coffee without the caffeine? It would be like a jam doughnut without the jam, or a Cheeseburger without the cheese. What a strange world we live in!

The girl then proceeded to ask, "Do you want French, Italian, Colombian, Java, Mexican, Indian, Kenyan, Ethiopian, Arabian or Greek coffee"

To which I replied, "I don't care, I just want a cup of coffee!"

I thought that was it, I was finally going to get my cup of coffee. But no, there was still more questions to follow. "Do you want your coffee black, or with fully skimmed, semi skimmed, full fat milk or cream?"

Finally I have my cup of coffee, and the world is a better place again. Next week I have enrolled in an evening class on 'How to order coffee in New York'! Anyway, enough of my mad ramblings, there is a certain Project 2067 to focus on. I thought that after the blood curdling UL's of the last section, it was time to bring back some light-hearted humour into our lives. So come out from behind the sofa, and prepare yourself for some side-splitting exploits and mishaps.

So, while I finish my sacred cup of coffee, and try and flag down a yellow cab to get back to my office, I want you to sit back and relax, and let the madness commence!

JUST FOR LAUGHS

NAME: Fart In The Dark
CODE: CM1601
ORIGIN: Unknown
STATUS: Undecided

Fart In The Dark

A man hurried back home from work one evening, so he could celebrate his birthday with his wife. As he drove home he felt a bit bloated and uncomfortable, which he put down to the birthday drink he had at lunchtime with his work mates. Lager always gave him indigestion!

When he arrived home his wife was there to greet him, gave him a birthday kiss and wished him happy birthday. She then gave him a blindfold and asked her husband to put it on as she had a surprise, which he obliged in doing so. His wife then escorted him into the dinning room of their house, and sat him down. Just as she had done this the telephone rang and she asked him not to peep while she answered it.

Now feeling so bloated he thought he was going to burst, he couldn't hold it in much longer. As soon as he heard his wife leave the room, he decided to let rip and performed the noisiest fart he had ever heard. Not only that, it also stank like rotten eggs! Now feeling relieved, he leant slightly to one side and let out a few smaller ones, thinking to himself that it was lucky the telephone rang.

After a few minutes, his wife came back into the room and asked him if he had peeped, which he replied he hadn't. She then took his blindfold off, and twelve people from around the table, all family and friends, shouted "Surprise!"

Summary

A funny, yet believable story; I am sure everyone reading this has an embarrassing tale to tell, like farting loudly in a crowded lift or during school assembly! Can you imagine the embarrassment the husband must have felt when he realised all his friends and family had been watching him all along in complete silence, so not to spoil the surprise?

Final Thoughts

This UL has gained popularity and has circulated on a grand style with the use of faxes and E-Mails. Although featuring in the book 'The Heart is a Lonely Hunter' by Carson Mc Culler in 1940, this UL cannot be traced to its origins.

JUST FOR LAUGHS

NAME: The College Letter
CODE: CM1602
ORIGIN: 1960's USA
STATUS: Undecided

The College Letter

The following letter was sent by a girl in college back home to her parents (un-edited version):

Dear Mum and Dad,

It has been three months since I left for college. I have been remiss in writing and I am very sorry for my thoughtlessness in not having written before. I will bring you up to date now, but before you read on, please sit down. You are not to read any further unless you are sitting down, okay.

Well then, I am getting along pretty well now. The skull fracture and the concussion I got when I jumped out of the window of my dormitory when it caught fire shortly after my arrival are pretty well healed now. I only spent two weeks in the hospital and now I can see almost normally and only get those headaches once a day.

Fortunately, an attendant at the gas station near the dorm witnessed the fire in the dormitory and my jump, and he was the one who called the fire dept. and the ambulance. He also visited me at the hospital and since I had nowhere to live because of the burnt out dormitory, he was kind enough to invite me to share his apartment with him. It's really a basement room, but it's kind of cute. He is a very fine boy and we have fallen deeply in love and are planning to get married. We haven't set the exact date yet, but it will be before my pregnancy begins to show.

Yes, mum and dad, I am pregnant. I know how very much you are looking forward to being grandparents, and I know you will welcome the baby and give it the same love and devotion you gave me when I was a child. The reason for the delay in our marriage is that my boyfriend has a minor infection, which prevents us from passing our premarital blood tests, and I carelessly caught it from him. This will soon clear up with the penicillin injections I am now taking daily.

I know you will welcome him into the family with open arms. He is kind, and although not well educated, he is ambitious. Although he is of a different race and religion to ours, I thought your oft-expressed tolerance would not permit you to be bothered by the fact that his skin colour is somewhat darker than ours. I am sure you will love him as I do. His family background is good too, for I am told his father is an important gun bearer in the village in Africa from which he comes.

Now that I have brought you up to date, I want to tell you there was no dormitory fire; I did not have a concussion or skull fracture; I was not in hospital; I am not pregnant; I am not engaged. I do not have syphilis, and there is no boyfriend in my life. However, I am getting a D in sociology and an F in Science; and I wanted you to see these marks in proper perspective.

Your loving daughter

Summary

This letter is hugely popular on the UL circuit, and has to go down as one of my favourites. Although very funny and witty, this letter intelligently plays on the parent's fears and attitudes towards college life. The tables are cleverly turned to stifle the impact of the real problems, bad grades! An elaborate story is told to put the bad grades into proper prospective.

This version of the letter is from 1968, and although there are many different versions, they all have the same structure. The only difference normally being the grades and the subjects to which the girl is taking.

Final Thoughts

The truth of the letter is unknown, although it is popularly believed that it originated from the 1960's. This is when college life went through some radical changes, and rules on dormitory life became more lapse, meaning students had more freedom.

A variation of this letter was circulated by E-Mail in 1998. The main difference being, at the end of the letter it was signed 'Chelsea Clinton'!

JUST FOR LAUGHS

NAME: The Parisian Bellboy
CODE: CM1603
ORIGIN: Unknown
STATUS: Undecided

The Parisian Bellboy

An American family were on holiday travelling around Europe, when they spent a few days at a hotel in Paris. After spending the first day sightseeing, they returned wearily to their hotel room, only to find it had been broken into. After a frantic search to find out what had been taken, they realised with astonishment that nothing was missing. The only thing strange was that the spare camera had been taken out its case and left on the bed, and all their toothbrushes were lying in the sink. The father reported the break in to the Hotel Manager, and the family were relocated to another room. The Manager gave his apologies and told them that the Bellboy was seen leaving their room. He went on to explain that it had been the Bellboy's last day and that he was probably trying to play a prank, he probably got disturbed in the act and left the room.

The American family went on to enjoy the rest of their trip around Europe, and thought nothing more of the Paris incident until they got home. When their photos were developed, they looked at them in disgust. At least ten of the photos were of the Bellboy taking pictures of himself in the Bathroom's mirror of the Hotel room. In each photo he was naked, grinning, and had one of their toothbrushes rammed firmly up his bum!

Summary

This story is enough to make anyone cringe. I am sure I don't have to tell you that the American family must have cleaned their teeth with these toothbrushes throughout the whole trip, oblivious to where they had been! This story does have other versions, but they normally involve an American family, and the hotel is normally in Paris. Why Paris? I suppose the French are an easy target, with the stereotyping of the French being unfriendly and having a low tolerance attitude towards foreigners (especially the Americans!).

Final Thoughts

This UL is a typical 'happened to a friend of a friend'; with most people believing it actually happened. I am not saying it didn't happen, and I would say that this story is quite believable. Other versions of this UL have been set in the Rocky Mountains of Canada, and most recently an American family holidaying in Mexico.

JUST FOR LAUGHS

```
NAME:     Stand Off At Sea
CODE:     CM1604
ORIGIN:   Unknown
STATUS:   False
```

Stand Off At Sea

Two radio operators, one of them aboard a U.S. Navy ship, had the following exchange:

Radio 1: Please divert your course 15 degrees to the north to avoid a collision.

Radio 2: Recommend you divert YOUR course 15 degrees.

Radio 1: This is the captain of a U.S. Navy ship. I say again, divert your course.

Radio 2: No, I say again, divert YOUR course.

Radio 1: This is an aircraft carrier of the U.S. Navy. This is a large warship. Divert your course now!

Radio 2: This is a lighthouse. Your call.

Summary

This UL, although false, is a story that the US Navy undoubtedly would like to shake off. This embarrassing tale was supposedly recorded by the Chief Of Navel Operations in 1995, although the UL has been around for at least twenty years. The operator in the warship, with his arrogant, pompous and self-righteous attitude, is pleasingly outwitted by the 'matter of fact', deadpan wit of the lighthouse operator.

Final Thoughts

Although this UL is documented as being about twenty years old, many researchers believe it goes back a lot further than that. Copies of this story are believed to have been passed around the US Navy in the 1960's as a joke.

PROJECT 2067

```
NAME:    The Cat Flap
CODE:    CM1605
ORIGIN:  Big Issue Magazine
STATUS:  False
```

The Cat Flap

In Germany, a man named Gunther Burpus (41) of Bremen, remained stuck in his cat flap for two days because passers by thought it was a modern art exhibition!

After mislaying his keys, Mr Burpus decided he would try and reach the handle of the front door to the house via the cat flap. He managed to get his head and shoulders in the cat flap before realising he was completely wedged in. He called out for help, which attracted the attention of a group of youths. Instead of helping him, they pulled down his trousers and pants, before running off laughing. They returned shortly afterwards with a can of paint, and painted Mr Burpus's bottom bright blue. To add a finishing touch, they stuck a daffodil between his buttocks. Before leaving, the youths erected a sign reading *'Germany Resurgent, an essay in street art- please give generously'*.

Passers by thought that Mr Burpus's screams for help was just an act and part of the exhibition. Mr Burpus was only freed after two days, when an old lady complained to the police and they came and set him free. Mr. Burpus explained to the police "I was shouting for help, but people kept saying 'very good, it's very clever!' and kept throwing coins down for me!"

Summary

This UL is funny, and disturbing at the same time. It plays on a fear that everybody possess; having to rely on the 'goodness of mankind' when needing help in a serious situation. We would all like to think that if it came to it, strangers would help if you needed it. In this story the opposite happened; and the passers by were too ignorant or stupid to realise that Mr. Burpus really needed help. This UL pokes a sharp stick at modern society!

Final Thoughts

This UL originated from a copy of the *Big Issue*, a magazine for homeless people, and spread quickly across the Internet, TV and the radio. Other magazines and newspapers also printed the story. The tale of Mr. Burpus is false, as no record can be found of it actually happening. Even from the German newspaper that supposedly reported on the story, had no record of it actually being printed.

PROJECT 2067

NAME: **The Biscuit Bullet**
CODE: **CM1606**
ORIGIN: **1995**
STATUS: **False**

The Biscuit Bullet

One scorching hot day a woman pulled into a parking space outside of the local supermarket. As she got out of her car, she noticed that a woman in a car next to hers was slumped over the steering wheel holding the back of her head. She felt concerned for the other woman, but carried on with her shopping regardless. One hour later she returned to the car, only to see that the woman was still in her car in the same position.

Now feeling very concerned, she went over to the car and tapped on the window, asking if the woman was alright.

The woman in the car replied in a panic stricken voice "Please call 999, I have been shot and I can feel my brains coming out!"

The woman at the window noticed a grey substance oozing out between the woman's fingers from the back of her head. With this, she fumbled for her mobile phone in her handbag, and called for help.

When the Ambulance arrived they carefully pried the woman's fingers away from her head and examined the injury. After a couple of minutes, the paramedics burst out laughing. After they managed to regain control of themselves, they explained that the heat had caused a packet of biscuit dough (which was lying on the top of the shopping bag) to explode. The metal lid of the packet had struck the woman on the back of the head, and the dough had shot out and stuck to her hair.

The sales receipt for the woman's shopping had shown that she had been sitting there in that position for two hours, before anyone offered to help! The manager of the Supermarket gave her a new tin of biscuit dough.

Summary

This is yet another humorous UL that gives modern society a dig in the ribs. If this story was true, it is unbelievable that the woman was in the car that long before anyone bothered to help. Also, the fact that the woman immediately thought she had been shot with no other explanation, was a sign of the times we live in. Mind you, it would seem very plausible at the time. She would have heard the biscuit tin explode and immediately felt the metal cap hit her on the back of her head. Her reaction would be to immediately put her hands on the back of her head, where she would have felt the hot dough oozing through her fingers thinking it was her brains!

Final Thoughts

The origin of this UL is very shady, although it became very popular in the US in 1995. That year had a very long hot summer, and during this time the story spiralled out of control. Although told as a true story, it became a popular joke circulating around the Internet. The story of a 'leaky brain' is nothing new, and this modern UL may be an offshoot of popular myths from days gone by.

PROJECT 2067

```
NAME:      The Bricklayer
CODE:      CM1607
ORIGIN:    1930's
STATUS:    Undecided
```

The Bricklayer

A Bricklayer working on a 3 storey high chimney had set up a pulley system so that he could raise the bricks up to where he was working. Although this was a good idea, he found that pulling the bricks up in this manner too exhausting. Just then another contractor had some material delivered and it was placed on the roof by a forklift brought to unload it. The bricklayer seized the opportunity and managed to get the driver to lift the bricks up onto the roof as well.

After finishing the job he had a lot of bricks left over, and decided to use the pulley system to take them down. First, he climbed down and attached a large metal bucket onto the rope and raised it up to the roof. Then he tied the other end of the rope to a railing, and climbed back up to the roof. He loaded all the bricks into the bucket, and climbed back down to the ground. He knew that the bricks would be heavy, so he wrapped the rope around his hand before untying it from the railing. What he didn't realise was how heavy the bricks were going to be, and as soon as he had untied the rope he shot up into the air at high speed. As he sped up into the air, he collided with the bucket of bricks that was plummeting towards earth. Now dazed, confused, and with a broken shoulder, he hit his head on the top of the pulley. At that precise moment, the bucket of bricks hit the ground and the load spilled over. What goes up must come down, and with the bucket now empty, he fell back down towards the ground hitting the empty bucket en-route. The bucket got wedged in-between his legs hurting his groin, and momentarily halting his descent. The bricklayer managed to struggle free and continued his fall. He landed on the pile of bricks on the ground and broke his ankle. Although in great pain, he felt lucky to be alive. He freed the rope from his hand and cried out for help. He heard a whizzing noise and looked up, just before the empty bucket hit him on the head!

```
Summary
```

What a strange world we live in when we find such great pleasure in other peoples misfortunes. I guess one of the reason being is that no matter how bad your day is, you know that somebody else has had it worse, and in a weird way that makes you feel better inside. Anyway, it is funny as long as it doesn't happen to you!

You couldn't have had much of a worse day than this particular bricklayer, although it was a basic mistake that led to the series of events. Instead of bringing the bricks down a little at a time, he thought he would defy logic and science and pull down a load that weighs more than his own body weight. Gravity took over from there!

Final Thoughts

This popular UL has been around for at least 70 years, as comedians have used the story since the 1930's. The Bricklayer has also popped up in many novels and films over the years.

PROJECT 2067

```
NAME:     The Naked Skier
CODE:     CM1608
ORIGIN:   1970's
STATUS:   Unknown
```

The Naked Skier

A young married couple were on their first day of a skiing holiday in Austria. The girl had forgot to go to the toilet before they had left the hotel, and by the time she had got off the ski lift on top of the slope, she was absolutely bursting. Her husband suggested that she skied half way down and relieves herself in the woods by the side of the slope, as no one would see her there.

The wife took up her husband's suggestions and skied down the slope and partially into the woods. She quickly pulled down her ski trousers and knickers and squatted over. In her rush to relieve herself as quickly as possible so no one else would see, she forgot to position her skis in the stop position. Suddenly she started moving backwards and was unable to stop. She skied backwards and out of control through the trees and out onto the ski slope, picking up speed all the while. Down the slope she continued, with her trousers and pants still down by her ankles, and her bare bottom out on show for everyone to see. Still out of control, the girl collided into a post for the ski lift and injured her ankle. It was a few minutes before her husband skied down to her and pulled up her trousers to save her from even more embarrassment.

After reaching the hospital, the girl started chatting to a man who was sitting next to her in the casualty ward. "Why are you in here?" she asked.

To which the man replied "I was skiing down the slope, admiring the view. When all of a sudden a girl skiing backwards while pulling a moony sped past me. In shock, I lost control and crashed into a tree, breaking my arm!"

Summary

Another embarrassing tale of a misfortunate soul, who really was caught out while on the piste! This is a very popular UL, and it is not hard to see why. This tale has the basic ingredient that all UL's must have; it's almost too good to be true. Although the 'humbug' part of you dismisses the truth of the story immediately, another part of you could quite easily see how it *could* happen.

JUST FOR LAUGHS

There are various versions of this UL, but the basis structure always remains the same. The location of the ski holiday depends on which side of the Atlantic the story is being told. The British versions are normally situated on mainland Europe, where the American versions tend to stick to the USA or Canada.

Final Thoughts

Still wearing it's huge collars and flares; this UL has come strutting straight out of the 70's. It is unclear which side of the Atlantic this story originated from, as it's popularity exploded in both America and Britain at the same time. Although, the American version believes it had been reported in a New Orleans newspaper, this never happened.

PROJECT 2067

```
NAME:     Take The Tube
CODE:     CM1609
ORIGIN:   Unknown
STATUS:   False
```

Take The Tube

A man working in a small office in the City of London felt very agitated when the large florescent tube, which was lighting his office, burnt out and needed changing. He immediately went down to the local electrical shop and bought a new one, replacing the burnt out tube when he returned. Now that he could see what he was doing again, he had to work hard to make up for loss time.

After a hard day slogging away, the man packed up and was ready for the journey home, when he suddenly remembered the florescent tube. He decided to take it home with him, as he could bung it in a skip that a neighbour had loaned. So he started his journey home travelling on the London Underground. The carriage he boarded was packed, so the man had to stand, holding the tube vertically in front of him.

As the journey progressed, more and more commuters boarded the train. Thinking that the florescent tube was a pole to hold onto, people grasped hold of it for balance. When it was the man's stop, several people still had hold of the tube, so he shrugged, let go, and stepped off the train.

Summary

This short and witty UL explains the way of modern city life in a nutshell. The pace of life is fast, sacrificing individuality for the soulless melting pot that is commonly known as the *rat race*. People are too busy racing around from 'a' to 'b' to care about anyone, or their surroundings. This selfish, unobservant attitude is highlighted in this UL, with the commuters on the underground not noticing they are actually holding a florescent tube and not the pole. Although this version is situated in London, it could have been situated at any modern cosmopolitan city in the world.

Final Thoughts

Not a very well known UL, and doesn't seem to travel well. It is believed to be originated in the US, and seldom heard this side of the Atlantic. It was originally thought to have appeared in a section of Readers Digest called 'Life In These United States', although that is not confirmed. The most popular version of this tale is situated on the Subway in Manhattan, New York City.

PROJECT 2067

```
NAME:     The Unzipped Fly
CODE:     CM1610
ORIGIN:   1950's
STATUS:   False
```

The Unzipped Fly: Version 1

A lady got in her car to do the weekly shopping but the car wouldn't start. Her husband told her to use his car and he would have a go at fixing the problem, which she did. When she returned from the shopping trip she saw that her husband was working on her car. With just his legs protruding out from underneath the car she thought that she would have a little fun with him. She bent down and unzipped his fly, slipped her hand in and gave a little squeeze. Giggling to herself, the lady entered her house and was shocked to see her husband sitting at the breakfast table reading a newspaper.

Horrified, the lady stammered, "Who's under my car?"

The husband explained that the problem was beyond his knowledge of cars and that he had to call the local mechanic.

When the lady had gathered her nerves, she explained to her husband the little prank she had pulled. They both rushed out into the drive and found the mechanic lying unconscious in a pool of blood underneath the car. The mechanic had hit his head on the underside of the car when he had reacted in shock when his fly was unzipped.

999 was called and an ambulance was quick to arrive on the scene. The paramedics were carrying the mechanic on a stretcher back to the ambulance when one of them asked what had happened. When they were told the story they laughed so much that they dropped the stretcher and in the fall the mechanic broke his arm.

The Unzipped Fly: Version 2

A young couple in Manchester drove their car to the local supermarket when their car started juddering just as they entered the car park. The girl went into the supermarket while her boyfriend decided to try and fix the car. When the girl returned she saw that a small group of people had gathered around the car.

When she got nearer she saw that a pair of male legs were protruding from under the chassis. Although the man was wearing shorts he was obviously not wearing any underwear as his bits were hanging loose for all to see. Feeling embarrassed for her boyfriend, she knelt down and tucked his bits back into his shorts. When she stood up she found herself face to face with her boyfriend who was standing, watching, over the other side of the bonnet. The mechanic had to have 5 stitches in his head.

Summary

Version 1 is similar to the original versions that have been dated back to the 1950's. *Version 2* on the other hand was collected on the Internet in 2002 and is one of the latter variants. These variations are only two of many, but can be considered as the norm' amongst them all. Versions do not tend to differ too much, although the mechanic is sometimes swapped for a Plummer working under a sink.

The Unzipped Fly is part of a larger collection of UL's that can be categorised as Sexual Embarrassments. We often find these types of stories as hilarious as we can identify with the embarrassment. It is like laughing at funny stories of other peoples misfortunes, we laugh because it makes us feel that our lives are not so bad. In the same way, we laugh at other peoples embarrassing situations because it helps us to cope with our own embarrassments.

Final Thoughts

This UL is popular because it is basic. The role-play situations may differ, but the motifs of the legend always remain apparent. The amount of stitches in the mechanics head varies, but it probably works out as one stitch for each month that has passed since he had last experienced that kind of foreplay!

CRIME...

INTRODUCTION...PAGE 50

THE STING...PAGE 51

THE BODY IN THE BED...PAGE 53

GRANDMA...PAGE 55

THE TELEPHONE SCAM...PAGE 58

THE SLASHER UNDER THE CAR................................PAGE 60

THE SUPERMARKET SCAM...PAGE 62

INFECTED NEEDLES..PAGE 64

THE KIDNEY HEIST..PAGE 67

RAZORBLADES IN WATERSLIDES...........................PAGE 69

Monday, 15th August
16.00 hrs: Back at the Office

CATEGORY: CRIME

I have just had the cab journey from hell! In between honking his horn and cursing fellow drivers and pedestrians alike, the cab driver bombarded me with his views on how to set the world to rights. Everything from world economics, to why soccer is not a sport for *real men.* I had to bite my lip on that last comment. Although I did wonder out loud what a *real man's* sport entailed. Does it involve wearing so much padding that you look like a Sumo wrestler with a crash helmet on your head? Or does it involve stopping the game every few minutes so everyone can have a rest and not tire each other out? My comments flew right over his head, as he continued his rant on to why Americans should only buy cars that are made in America.

The journey was not completely wasted though as I think I have the answer to one of the greatest questions of all time: Who were the three wise men? I think they must have been New York cabbies! Their information and knowledge seems to hold no bounds, and they will have an opinion on any subject you could possibly think of.

Anyway, the journey from hell took more time than I anticipated and I have arrived back at the office (shoebox) a little late. We still have a whole file to go through before joining the rat race for the daily battle of going home.

After looking on the bright side of life, we turn our attention to the more sinister subject of crime. No matter what walk of life you come from, crime plays a dominant part in our everyday lives. With the technology of surveillance and security getting increasingly sophisticated, criminals are having to think of ingenious ways to beat the law. Of course, not all criminals are masterminds. Judging by some exploits, some of them must have thought God had said 'Trains' when he/she was giving out brains, and asked for a slow one! In other words, they are one can short of a six-pack when it comes to the brain department.

The following legends contain the good, the bad, and the most unbelievable criminal capers. But before carrying on, remember crime *doesn't* pay. Unless you live in America, and play a professional sport that is!

CRIME

```
NAME:     The Sting
CODE:     CR1701
ORIGIN:   Unknown
STATUS:   Unknown
```

The Sting

A friend of mine was driving home one evening, when he decided to stop off at a shop and buy a newspaper. As he pulled up outside of the shop, he noticed that he had parked on a double yellow line. Afraid of getting a parking fine, he decided to dart into the shop while leaving his hazard lights on and the engine still running, knowing that he would be quick. Not quick enough though, as my friend returned to find the car had been stolen. Realising he had also left his wallet in the glove box, he quickly informed the police and filed a report. He returned home late that evening and informed his wife to what had happened.

A couple of days later my friend leaves his house to catch the bus to work, only to find the missing car sitting in the driveway. Astounded, he walks over to the car and notices an envelope placed on the drivers seat. He opens the envelope and reads the note inside:

Dear Sir,

I apologise from the bottom of my heart for taking your car. My wife went into labour and I panicked, stealing your car so I could take her to hospital. I know it was the wrong thing to do, and I would like to offer you the following as compensation for the inconvenience caused. Enclosed are four tickets to the FA Cup Final. The tickets are for the exclusive section, and are excellent seats. I hope you enjoy the game, and find it in your heart to forgive me.

Being a huge football fan, my friend was very exited about the prospect of seeing the biggest match in the football calendar. He immediately ran back into his house to tell his wife and two sons that they are all going to see the FA Cup Final.

The day arrives and the family set off to see the match. After an exciting and thrilling game, the family arrive back home only to find that they had been robbed. The whole house is virtually empty!

They realised that they had been conned. The car thief had lured the family away from the house, knowing that they would be out all day. The thief had obtained my friends address from his wallet left in the glove box. The wallet also contained the photos of his two kids and his wife, so he knew that he had to get four tickets. The car thief guessed that they were all huge football fans from the football stickers and novelties in the car.

Summary

The theft of the car is purely opportunitist, but the thief seizes on the opportunity to spin an elaborate sting on the poor unsuspecting family. The gullibility of the man in question is probably caused by the excitement of receiving the FA Cup Final tickets. Any normal person would smell a rat a mile off, but then again, any man who leaves his car running with his wallet inside doesn't have his lift going up to the top floor - if you know what I mean!

Final Thoughts

Although the story doesn't seem plausible, it certainly could have happened. After all, professional con men make a living from the gullibility of the human nature.

CRIME

```
NAME:      The Body In The Bed
CODE:      CR1702
ORIGIN:    US, Early 1990's
STATUS:    True
```

The Body In The Bed

A young couple checked into a prestigious hotel in Las Vegas. After entering the executive suite, they both noticed a putrid smell coming from their room. They immediately went down to the reception and demanded for their room to be cleaned. A maid was sent up to the suite while the couple enjoyed complementary drinks at the hotel bar.

After the maid had finished, the couple went back to the suite only to find that the room still smelt foul. Again, the couple complained at reception, and again, Housekeeping was notified. While the room was being cleaned for the second time, the young couple went for a walk along the strip.

After returning to their suite, they were immediately met by the same foul odour. Housekeeping was yet again called up to the room, and with the couple investigated the source of the smell. They traced it back to the king size bed, and to the mattress itself. After ripping open the mattress, they found the decomposing body of a man.

Apparently, the body belonged to a well-known gangster and playboy in Las Vegas. It is believed that he had been 'hit' because of a long-term feud between rival gangster families.

As part of an incentive to keep quiet about the whole affair, the management of the hotel offered the young couple complimentary stay in the hotel for life.

Summary

This legend first appeared in the early 1990's, and has many different versions. Although, all the versions have the same story structure and changes are only minor. Most versions are situated in Las Vegas, but the actual Hotel name changes from story to story. Sometimes the victim is a prostitute and is found in a cut out hollow under the bed.

This gruesome UL doesn't appear to have any hidden agenda's; it is told purely to shock people. Las Vegas was is a notorious haunt for gangsters, and the Hotels could seem a fitting location for such grizzly and shady criminal activities

Final Thoughts

This UL is rated as *true*. Although a case like this has never been reported to have happened in Las Vegas, many similar incidents have happened across the US. A spate of similar cases occurred in the mid 1990's, after the UL had become widespread. The UL could have originated from an incident that happened in 1988 in a motel in Minneola, New York. The body of a girl was found in the bedspring of the bed after at least a couple of guests had stayed in the room and complained about the smell. The earliest reported incident of this kind dates back to 1982.

CRIME

```
NAME:     Grandma
CODE:     CR1703
ORIGIN:   Europe, During WW2
STATUS:   False
```

Grandma: Version 1

A family from London decided to drive to the south of France for a camping trip. Grandma wasn't feeling too well, and the rest of the family were apprehensive on taking Grandma on the long drive with them. But Grandma ensured them all that she would be all right, and besides, she had been looking forward to the trip.

After the long journey, they finally arrived at their destination and began to set up the tents. Grandma had her own tent, while the rest of the family shared the other one. After a good nights sleep, the father entered Grandma's tent to wake her up. He quickly realised something was wrong and discovered that she had died during the night.

Now in shock, the family decided to cancel the rest of their trip and to drive back home immediately. After much discussion, the father decided that they would take Grandma back with them in the car. Having Grandma's body flown home separately would be too costly with too much paper work involved. Besides, they were in a foreign country and believed the legal procedures would take too long.

Grandma's body had stiffened and had begun to smell, so they wrapped up her body in one of the tents and tied the package to the roof rack. When this had been done, they began their miserable journey home. The family were apprehensive about being stopped by customs. How would they explain having a dead body wrapped up on the roof rack? They had no need to worry. When they had crossed the channel, they were allowed to drive straight through customs without being stopped.

Still a couple of hours away from home, they decided to stop for a break, and have something to drink and eat. They returned from the café only to find their car missing. It had been stolen along with Grandma.

They never saw their car or Grandma again!

PROJECT 2067

Grandma: Version 2

A family were travelling by car across the Californian desert. The family consisted of the father, mother, two children and Grandma. During the journey Grandma fell very sick and within an hour had died. The father decided it would be too distressing for the kids to keep Grandma in the car, so he decided to wrap her up in a blanket and secure her to the roof rack.

After three hours of driving, they reached a small town on the outskirts of Arizona. The father pulled up into a petrol station, so he could use the phone so he could report Grandma's death and sort out some details. The rest of the family got out of the car to buy drinks and to stretch their legs.

When they all returned they found that the car had been stolen, along with Grandma strapped to the roof. Both the car and Grandma were never seen again.

Because there was no body to prove that Grandma had died, it took years for the insurance of her death to come through.

Summary

I have given two examples of this famous UL; to illustrate the different perceptions of the legend depending on which country you heard it in. *Version 1* is the British version, and concentrates on the difficulties of being in a foreign country under these circumstances. The family's main concern is to carry Grandma's body back to their homeland, without being stopped by French officials or British customs. This is because the family know too well of all the red tape that would be involved if the death had been reported in France, let alone the time and cost involved.

Version 2 is the American version, and has a completely different outlook to the problems involved. The main reason for wrapping Grandma on the roof is to not upset the children. Also, being as they are driving through a desert, I imagine the car would get very hot and Grandma's body might have started to smell a little! The main difference between the two versions of the legend is that in the American version, worrying about crossing a border between countries and customs in not an issue.

Anyway, the action taken to the situation of Grandma's death is the same in both examples. The conclusion to the tale is also the same, with the car and Grandma being stolen, never to be seen again.

Final Thoughts

In it's present form, this UL can be dated back to Europe, during World War 2 (1939-1945). Possibly originating from stories of families attempting to cross European borders to escape the Nazis.

Some Folklorists believe that the legend goes back even further. In one-way or other, embedded in 17th and 18th century folklore.

PROJECT 2067

NAME: The Telephone Scam
CODE: CR1704
ORIGIN: USA, late 1990's
STATUS: True

The Telephone Scam

A warning chain message was sent via E-Mail and Faxes, similar to the following:

Warning!

Con artists are phoning businesses and residents claiming to be BT service engineers. They claim to be testing your line and ask you to dial 90# (nine – zero – gate) on your telephone. Once you have dialled the numbers, the con artist has access to your phone line and is able to make long distance telephone calls that are then charged to your account.

This scam could cost you and your business thousands of pounds and needs to be taken seriously. Please inform colleagues, friends and family of this fraud.

If you receive such a call, ask the engineer for his name and a call back number. Then hang up. It is important to note that a telephone engineer would never ask a customer to help check a telephone line by dialling any numbers.

Please pass this information on.

Summary

Although I have marked this UL's status as 'True', there are some aspects that have been exaggerated. The main diversity from reality in the UL is that resident phone lines have never been affected by this scam. Telephone fraud of this kind, is normally directed at businesses using networked PBX systems.

Also, the number that is dialled to give access to the line would vary depending on the PBX equipment that is being used. The con artist is simply gaining access to the outside line, so the number that needs to be dialled depends on what number your equipment uses to transfer the call for an outside line.

Final Thoughts

There has been other telephone scams, the latest being with mobile phones. Apparantly, if you dial a certain number before dialling the actual number you want to ring, you receive a free phone call. This is because mobile phone technicians use the code to gain access to the line.

PROJECT 2067

```
NAME:     The Slasher Under The Car
CODE:     CR1705
ORIGIN:   USA, 1950's
STATUS:   False
```

The Slasher Under The Car: Version A

Last Christmas, a lady carried her shopping back to her car which was parked in the multi-storey car park. She placed her shopping on the ground and fumbled in her purse for the car key. Just as the lady had found her key, a man hiding underneath her car slashed both her ankles with a knife. The lady fell to the ground in such agony and shock, she was unable to scream. The man crawled swiftly out from under the car, grabbed her purse and shopping, and casually walked off.

The Slasher Under The Car: Version B

As part of a gang initiation ritual, a woman's body part has to be collected and produced to the rest of the gang. The only rule is that this has to be carried out in a well-lit area. As this ritual normally happens at night, petrol stations are an obvious target. The assailant targets lone women and hides under their car when they are paying for the petrol. When the lone female comes back to her car, the attacker slashes her ankles with a knife. When she falls to the ground, the attacker cuts off a body part and runs off. The bigger the body part, the more recognition the gang member receives!

Summary

There are many different versions to this UL, and many are told as formal warnings. *Version A* is of the more traditional format, which has been told since the 1950's. Similar stories to this have been told in almost every Mall in every state of America, all of them being told as an actual event that has happened! The story is very believable, as Christmas shoppers are vulnerable targets for muggers with all the expensive gifts that have been bought. This legend may have been originally used as a direct warning to woman, to be vigilant when alone.

CRIME

Version B has a more sinister under tone, with the threat of gang initiation rituals similar to *Lights Out* (HR4707). The threat of an attacker waiting for the lone woman to get back to her car is similar to the *Backseat Hitchhiker* (HR4701).

Both UL's have the same hidden moral agenda, raising questions about the vulnerability of lone woman. This UL was born in a time when attitudes towards women were changing. No longer did woman accept the role of the good little housewife whose only goal in life was to please her man. Girls wanted more freedom, to go out and have a laugh. Some people found this new attitude threatening, and it is possible these legends were used as scare tactics.

Time moves on, and the moral issues of the 1950's are no longer relevant. So the UL mutates with the changing times, and a new version is born (*Version B*). This time it incorporates a different fear of modern society; Mindless violence.

Final Thoughts

Although the first recorded case of *The Slasher Under The Car* was from the 1950's, the legend didn't hit its peak popularity until the mid 1980's.

PROJECT 2067

```
NAME:     The Supermarket Scam
CODE:     CR1706
ORIGIN:   Unknown
STATUS:   False
```

The Supermarket Scam

A woman was carrying out her weekly shop in the local Supermarket, when she noticed an old lady staring at her. Wherever she moved in the shop, the old lady followed her. Feeling annoyed, the woman approached the old lady and told her to quit following her. The old lady apologised and sadly told the woman "You look so much like my daughter. Unfortunately she died a few months back, and I never got to say goodbye. I was too late arriving at the hospital, and she was already dead. I just wish I got to say goodbye!"

Now feeling awful for being so abrupt, the woman suggested that they carry on with their shopping together. The old lady thanked her, and told her she used to enjoy shopping with her daughter.

When they had finished their shopping, the old lady was first at the checkout till. As the shopping was getting rung up, the old lady turned to the woman and asked her "You are kind like my daughter was, and have been such a comfort. When I leave could you say 'Goodbye Mum' to me, I think it would go along way in easing my grieving?"

The woman although embarrassed by the request, couldn't find it in her heart to refuse the old lady. So when the old lady was leaving, the woman shouted "Goodbye Mum" and gave her a little wave.

When the woman's shopping was rung up, the cost of the bill horrified her. Pointing to her one bag of shopping, she told the cashier there must have been a mistake. The cashier told the woman that her mother had said that she was paying for both shopping loads.

The woman ran out into the car park, just in time to see the old lady driving away laughing out of the window.

Summary

This UL has many variants, but all carry the same message of mistrust. A person's good-hearted deed is always slapped back into their face, normally in the form of a bill. The locations of such scams do vary. Some versions are based in a roadside café, and normally involve a hitchhiker getting stuck with the bill after getting conned by a well-presented businessman who had picked him up. After lunch, the businessman informs the hitchhiker he needs to fill his car up with petrol, and to wait here and finish his coffee. The hitchhiker is also told to wave at the waitress so they know who he is with. The businessman doesn't return and…well, you can guess the rest!

Versions that are located in a supermarket, normally involve the same elaborate story used for the scam. Quite often, the relative who has died is a son of the old lady, but the same formula is used.

The way the scam plays on peoples good nature would be considered by many as low. This UL wants us to realise the depths some people will sink to just to get a free ride. Yet another satirical look at greed in modern society.

Final Thoughts

The popularity of this UL has gained momentum over the last decade, and the familiarity of the tale is widespread across the world. Versions of the legend crept into comedy sketches and film scenes throughout the nineties, the most famous being in the hit film 'Dumb and Dumber'.

PROJECT 2067

```
NAME:      Infected Needles
CODE:      CR1707
ORIGIN:    USA, 1930s
STATUS:    False
```

Infected Needles   Version 1

During the school holidays, a group of girls went to see a film at their local cinema. When one of the girls sat down into her seat, she felt something sharp poking into her. She immediately jumped up and found a syringe placed into the fold of the chair. Tied to the end of the syringe was a note with this message written on it, 'WELCOME TO THE REAL WORLD'.

The girl was rushed to the nearest hospital, and the syringe was immediately taken away to be tested. The results were, as the doctors had feared; the syringe needle was infected with HIV Positive.

Worryingly, this was not the first incident of its kind, and no doubt will not be the last. Please be extra careful before sitting down at the cinema.

Infected Needles   Version 2

Certain gangs are targeting clubbers with a unique and vicious hate campaign. Each member carries a wad of stickers, the stickers are round, yellow, and have the message 'Welcome To The Real World' written on them. The gang choose their victims at random, and once selected, a member sticks a sticker on the unaware clubber. The stickers are filled with minute needles infected with HIV Positive.

Many incidents have happened at nightclubs and bars all over the country, and the victims are truly chosen at random. Clubbers need to take extra care, especially when dancing within a crowded area.

Summary

The legend spans across a time scale of at least 70 years. The original versions are dated back to the early 1930's, and are similar to *Version 1*. The early versions were also based in Movie Theatres (cinemas), with the only real difference being the reason for being jabbed with a needle. In *Version 1*, the needle is maliciously left to deliberately infect a person with the deadly AIDS virus. AIDS was not known in the 1930's, so there was another sinister reason for being jabbed with a needle. In the 1930's, New Orleans, young girls were warned to beware of the 'Needle Man'. A man would sit either side of their young victim in the cinema; one man would then inject morphine into the young girl. Once the young girl was sedated, the two men would carry her out and she would be sold into slavery.

Version 1 originated from the late 1980's, when AIDS became a world epidemic. The media and the governments ran huge awareness campaigns to warn of the dangers of this killer disease. Of course, UL's thrive and feed from paranoia, mutating with the fears of the time. *Version 1* is probably a merger of two UL's. The original 1930's version (which has already been discussed) and *AIDS Mary*, which will be discussed later.

Dance music exploded onto the scene in the 1990's, bringing with it the 'clubbing' culture. Raves were rampant in Britain during the early 1990's, and drugs were closely associated with it. *Version 2* incorporates this new culture, and serves as a warning to clubbers to be careful. It also acts as a deterrent to keep people away from clubs. When this particular version was thriving during 1998, clubs were reporting a loss of revenue of up to 50%; people were simply staying away.

These versions of the legend thrive because of the fear everyone has for AIDS. The paranoia of the 1980's has died down, but everyone still knows the deadly danger of becoming HIV Positive.

Final Thoughts

Although the status of the UL is false, similar incidents have occurred over the years. In 1989, a group of teenagers (mainly girls) went on a terror spree in New York City, jabbing pins into the necks of females at random. They attacked 41 women in this way before they were caught. The main concern was that the pins might have been infected with HIV, this concern proved fruitless. The gang's reason for doing this was that it was a bit of a laugh, and just a game to them.

A similar incident happened on Rhode Island (US) in 1997, two medical students jabbed 32 of their colleagues in the arm for a prank (nice friends!).

In 1999, a woman in Maryland (US) was attacked at a petrol station. A man approached her and demanded money. She told him that she only had a dollar. He told her that would do, and pulled his arm around her and kissed her on her cheek. He then pricked her with a needle and said "Welcome to reality, you have HIV". The woman was not infected.

A big problem nowadays is that robbers are using (supposedly) HIV infected needles to threat and rob people. In Britain this is such a problem that there are calls for law to be changed, so that people convicted of these crimes will receive harsher penalties. After all, the physiological effect on the victims must be immense.

CRIME

```
NAME:     The Kidney Heist
CODE:     CR1708
ORIGIN:   USA 1991
STATUS:   False
```

The Kidney Heist

On a Friday evening after finishing work for the week, a man decided to go for a drink before heading off home. The man jumped on the tube and crossed London from the City to the West End, and entered a bar in Soho. Not long after arriving at the bar, a beautiful girl started chatting to him. They seemed to have hit it off and spent the whole evening drinking and chatting with each other. At the end of the evening the girl suggested that they go back to her hotel room where she was staying. The man couldn't believe his luck and promptly agreed.

After a short taxi ride they arrived at the hotel, and went straight up to the girls room. The girl poured a glass of wine for them both, and they both started to undress. Suddenly the man felt very drowsy and blacked out.

The man awoke the next day in the bathtub of the hotel room, submerged in ice. He couldn't move and hurt all over. On the wall was a note, which read 'If you want to live, dial 999 immediately'. A phone had been placed on a stool next to the bathtub, within his reach. He dialled 999 as instructed and was put through to a paramedic. He was asked if a tube had been inserted in his back, after feeling for it the man replied "Yes". The paramedic told the man to stay calm and perfectly still and that an ambulance was on its way.

The Paramedic knew straight away what had taken place, as it was not the first time it had happened. Sure enough, one of the man's kidneys had been removed by a highly professional gang that specialised in the smuggling of human organs. The girl had lured him to the hotel room where she had drugged him; the rest of the gang had been lying in wait.

Summary

This incredibly gruesome tale has been very popular since 1991, and has generated great interest from the media over the last decade. Stories of human organs being sold on the black market is nothing new, and the demand for them for medical research has led to some shady dealings in the past. I remember reading about the grave robbers that dug up dead bodies after they had been buried, and sold them to professors at Universities for this very purpose. In Mary Shelly's Frankenstein, the monster was made up of stolen body parts and organs.

The difference with this legend is the fact that the man was still alive when his kidney was stolen. He was lured into a trap, and a highly professional gang that knew exactly what they were doing carried out the whole exercise. After all, it would take a skilled surgeon to perform an operation to remove a kidney.

The man was easy prey for the pretty girl, as all men are! In his desperation and lust he let all his defences down. This legend plays out the fear of modern faceless cities, where you can't let your guard down for a second and you can't trust anyone. If you do, you could be the latest statistic on a crime sheet.

Final Thoughts

The latest versions of the legend differ from the original 1991 legends. In the original the man was always with a group of male friends, being lured away by the girl. The bath of ice and the note did not exist back then, as the man normally awoke in a bed and manages to ring his friends, who rush round to his aid.

Although this legend is false, true stories of human organ thieving keep cropping up. Early in 2001, certain British hospitals were under scrutiny, accused of removing organs from young children and babies who had died, without the consent of relatives!

In India 1998, three surgeons and seven other people were arrested for unlawfully removing body organs from unsuspecting victims. The gang targeted the unemployed, offering them job opportunities. All they had to do was to go for a medical. During the medical, surgeons would find a defect that required a minor operation. A Kidney would be removed during these operations to be resold on the black market without the victim even knowing. No job was offered to the victim after the operation.

The outcry caused by this case caused the Indian government to toughen its laws, but still in some regions the sale of body organs is commonplace.

CRIME

```
NAME:     Razorblades In Waterslides
CODE:     CR1709
ORIGIN:   Unknown
STATUS:   False
```

Razorblades In Waterslides

A water park in Walton (Surrey) was all the rage when I was young, and the hot summer of 1985 was no exception. A waterslide called the 'Black Hole' was everyone's favourite; a fast ride with an almost sheer drop in complete darkness.

However, during this particular summer, a certain story made people think twice about going there. Apparently, gangs of youths found it great fun to stop halfway down the slide (Black Hole) and stick razorblades to the sides with chewing gum. A girl aged 13 suffered serious injuries when her back and legs were cut due to the prank.

The story refused to die, and the Waterslide Park's popularity steadily declined. The effect on business was devastating, and shortly afterwards the park closed up for good.

Summary

When I was younger this story was taken as gospel, and it did stop kids wanting to go to the Water Park. It was not until I read an article on the Internet, that I actually realised it was a legend. The article told about an event (similar to the version above) happening in a place called 'Grundy's', which was an Amusement Park in Surfers Paradise (Australia). This supposedly happened in the late 1970's, and involved a girl (aged 12 or 13) being cut by a razorblade, stuck to the slide with chewing gum. Versions of the UL can also be found in almost every state in America.

This UL is particularly malicious, as it has had an impact on the business's involved. It is very believable that gangs would do this just for 'kicks', and the worrying thing is that the victim cannot do anything about it. The legend has an impact because it makes people feel very vulnerable. You can travel down a waterslide at great speed, and with little vision. The feeling of being out of control adds to the buzz of the ride, but this very feeling fuels the fear that this legend generates.

Final Thoughts

An American version situated in England, has an extra twist added to it. It states that water slides are now banned in Britain because of the risk factor involved due to that particular incident. This is not true.

ANIMALS & PESTS...

INTRODUCTION..PAGE 72

SPIDERS IN PLANTS...PAGE 74

THE SURREY PUMA...PAGE 76

COCKROACHES ON THE TONGUE............................PAGE 79

THE LOG FLUME HORROR...PAGE 81

THE IMPORTED SNAKE..PAGE 83

THE DEAD CAT PACKAGE..PAGE 86

ALLIGATORS IN THE SEWERS..................................PAGE 89

KASPER, THE WOODEN CAT.......................................PAGE 92

PROJECT 2067

Tuesday, 16th August
08.30hrs: Just arrived at the office

CATEGORY: ANIMALS & PESTS

What a beautiful morning! Today is going to be another hot one, but there is a slight breeze to take away the intensity of the heat. The subway trains were all running on time and were not overcrowded for once. The brisk walk to work was pleasant and I didn't get mugged, which is always a bonus! For some reason I feel refreshed, although I don't know why because I didn't get much sleep last night. The pressure is starting to get to me, the project was swirling around my mind like a tornado, and sucking up any other thoughts I might have had with it. After tossing and turning in bed for a few hours, I decided to watch some TV. Big mistake! Have you ever had the pleasure of watching American TV? If not, you don't know what you are missing. In fact, I can tell you what you have been missing; adverts, adverts, adverts. There are adverts before a half hour program, 30 seconds into one, halfway through one, and just before the end credits. They can make a 90-minute film last at least 2 hours!

"What about the choice of channels?" I hear you ask, "They have loads of channels". Sure, you could channel hop all night. In fact you probably would have to do so to find a decent program. Most channels fill your screen with pure rubbish, programs that have about as much interest as a trains convention in the local town hall. Boy, do I miss Match Of The Day on a Saturday night!

Lets now get straight to work, as we look at the UL subject of Animals & Pests. Animals have always played a major part in all forms of mythology, legends and religion. A popular subject matter of UL's is Snakes. The very word can make some people shudder, and are often portrayed throughout mythology as evil and conniving creatures. The Christian story of the Garden of Eden portrays the snake as the very symbol of evil and temptation, and they don't fair up to much in the legend of St. Patrick, where he was praised for ridding the whole of Ireland of these reptiles. Snakes in Greek mythology also have a rough ride, especially when famously acclaimed for giving the evil Medusa a bad hair day!

Not all mythology regard snakes as evil, and they were considered sacred among certain cultures. The Aztecs worshipped snakes, and the Aboriginals of Australia believed that a giant rainbow serpent was the creator of life. The Rock Python was considered sacred by some African cultures, and it was forbidden to kill them. Although snakes are regarded highly with these cultures and others, they are sadly back to the stereotype of 'Dr. Evil' when it comes to UL's.

ANIMALS & PESTS

Another popular animal of mythology throughout the times are Cats. The popular pet has had a varied reputation over the years that go from one extreme to another. Cats were worshiped by the ancient Egyptians, and were supposed to protect the living and the dead from evil. To the other extreme, cats in some legends are considered evil, especially when associated with witches and black magic.

Cat stories are very common in UL circles. In fact, some legends grouped as 'The Dead Cat' stories even have their own theme. Cats are a versatile subject for legends, as they are either loved or loathed by humans.

Another form of cat legends is the 'Big Cat' sightings, which are sightings of animals such as Pumas and Panthers in urban areas. This topic is covered in the research of Cryptozoology, which is the scientific study of hidden animals. Don't worry, I haven't lost the plot, Cryptozoology will be explained in greater detail in the summary of the UL *The Surrey Puma* (AN1602).

Finally, we have spiders. Spiders are a sure hit with the fear factor, and our eight legged friends are an essential ingredient to the world of UL's. These little creepy crawlies can strike fear in the hearts of the toughest of men, and transform them into snivelling babies. Even the mere sight of one in your bathtub, can put you off your bubble bath for weeks!

Now, we must get started, I have a brunch appointment with my boss who has just flown in from London. He is expecting a full progress report, and it better be good or he will pull the plug on the whole project. I am sure that my natural charm and developed communication skills will see me through. If that doesn't work, I will have to take Max to a bar tonight and get him so hammered that he will agree to anything!

PROJECT 2067

NAME: Spiders In Plants
CODE: AN1601
ORIGIN: Britain, Scandinavia, 1970s
STATUS: False

The Spider In the Yucca

A woman decided to buy a Yucca plant to brighten up her lounge. She saw a nice Yucca at the supermarket, and bought it while doing her weekly food shopping. After placing the Yucca near the window in her lounge, the woman began to water it. Suddenly, she heard a squeak. The woman stepped back, wondering where the noise came from. She heard it again, and this time she could tell it came directly from the plant itself.

The woman phoned the supermarket and explained about the noise. After being put on hold, a man came back on line and gave her the telephone number for Kew Gardens, telling her to phone them immediately.

The woman didn't waste any time in phoning Kew Gardens. After explaining the story again, she was told that an expert was being sent round to her house. In the meantime, she got told to vacate the house taking any children and family pets with her.

One hour later, a white van pulled up sharply into her drive. A man promptly got out and asked to be let into the house. A few minutes later the man reappeared with the Yucca plant and placed it into the back of the van, and quickly closed the doors.

Only then did the man explain what was going on. He told the woman that the squeaking noise that she had heard came from a Tarantula Spider that was nesting inside the Yucca plant.

The Spider In the Cactus

A lady bought a Cactus home from the local nursery. She had only had it half an hour when she saw it move. At first she thought it must have been her imagination, but then she saw it move again.

When she reported it to the local Nursery, they at first thought she was nuts. Only after the manager had come onto the phone, she was taken seriously. He told her to leave the house immediately and wait for an employee he was sending round.

The employee promptly arrived, and the lady showed him to where the Cactus was. He was just about to approach the Cactus, when it suddenly exploded, sprawling baby Tarantulas all over the carpet.

Summary

The popularity of imported plants such as Cactus during in the 1970's gave birth to this legend across Scandinavia and Britain. The British versions, such as *The Spider In The Yucca*, normally centre on the plant being bought at a brand named store or Supermarket. The versions told in and around London, often state that an expert from Kew Gardens was sent to deal with the problem.

The American versions such as *The Spider In The Cactus* didn't appear on the scene until the late 1980s. These legends falsely claimed that the plants were bought at *Franks Nursery*, a large Nursery chain in America.

The American versions do not differ much from the European ones. Sometimes Scorpions are found instead of Tarantulas, and the ending is normally more dramatic (the plant exploding releasing hundreds of the baby creatures).

Final Thoughts

This UL may be 30 years old, but I hear new and different versions all the time. Only a couple of months ago I was told that a Tarantula was found in a bunch of bananas, bought from Tescos!

The *Spiders In Plants* legends will spread and grow for many years because of one simple reason; the deep rooted fear that many people have about creepy crawlies (especially spiders!).

PROJECT 2067

```
NAME:      The Surrey Puma
CODE:      AN1602
ORIGIN:    Surrey, England 1959
STATUS:    Undecided
```

The Surrey Puma: Example 1

In August 1959, Mr A Burningham couldn't believe his eyes as he was driving along a country lane in Crondall one evening. Less than 50 metres ahead of him, an enormous great cat the size of a Labrador dog was crossing the road. Mr.Burningham pulled over and observed as the great cat crouched down below trees, watching lambs in the nearby field. After a while, the cat walked off and was out of sight. Mr Burningham continued on his journey home, not quite believing what he had just seen.

In fact, it wasn't until there was another sighting three years later (1962), that he actually reported what he had seen. The second sighting happened near Farnham in Surrey, and was reported in the local newspaper. Ernest Jellett was walking along a country lane to work at the Reservoir on the North Downs, when he saw a big black cat bounding towards him chasing a rabbit. Mr Jellet shouted out at the cat in surprise, and scared it off. The cat was described as having a round, flat face, a long thin tail, and big paws.

The police investigated the story and found a flattened patch of ground where a large animal may have rested. The sightings continued throughout the sixties, with big paw prints being found and strange howling noises heard at night.

The Surrey Puma: Example 2

The latest sighting of the Surrey Puma occurred in Guildford in October 2000, by Mr.Quelsh. The large cat was spotted lying on a running track at the Spectrum (a sports and leisure complex in Guildford, Surrey), 100 yards from where Mr.Quelsh was standing. Mr.Quelsh commented that ""It was twice the length of a domestic cat and had its tail curled up above the ground. It definitely wasn't a dog, and did not seem aggressive. It laid on the green for a few minutes and then walked off into the trees."

Summary

As you can see from the two examples, the Surrey Puma legend refuses to die. There are still sightings being recorded on a regular basis, 40 years on from the original. The first sighting was near the Surrey/Hampshire border, and most of the sightings since have occurred around the Guildford area. In such places as Cranleigh, Thursley, Godalming, and Guildford City.

Although the first sighting of the Surrey Puma was in 1962, it wasn't until 1964 that the legend really took off. Apart from weird howling noises heard at night, and big paw prints found across the county, other incidents also occurred. A flock of sheep stampeded out of a field, frightened by a strange animal. Nearby, a deer was found dead. Its body had been badly mauled and bitten. In 1966, a very blurred photo was taken supposedly of the Surrey Puma. The photo was so blurred it was hard to distinguish what animal it was, so can hardly be considered evidence.

The question is; if there is a Puma roaming the Surrey countryside, how did it get there and why? Also, why has the animal not been caught after 40 years? There are a few theories to these questions: One theory is that a Puma owned by a well-known female singer, was taken away at her own request at a Health Farm near Guildford. The Puma was taken in the early hours of the morning under the blanket of darkness and was driven away in a Horse Box, later to be released into woods.

Another theory is that domestic cats have been interbreeding with Scottish Wild Cats, creating a new species. Another wonderful theory is that the cats belong to a species that was supposed to be extinct. Big Cats are known to have roamed Britain in Prehistoric times, perhaps they never completely died out!

Final Thoughts

The Surrey Puma was not the first Big Cat sightings ever to have taken place, and it certainly will not be the last. Big Cat sightings are commonplace in American Folklore, with stories of the 'Motown Panthers' being one example of many. Back in England we also have the 'Exmoor Beast', and the 'Shooter Hill Cheetah' of South East London. The 'Shooter Hill Cheetah' sighting gained credibility because it was spotted by a policeman. This sighting combined with the stories of the 'Surrey Puma' sparked the notorious Cheetah Hunt of 1963. Scotland has also had their fair share of Big Cat sightings over the years.

Research into Big Cats is one of the many subjects under investigation by the study of Cryptozoology. Cryptozoology is the scientific study and investigation of animals that are unusual because of place and time. Also, when the evidence concerning their existence is insufficient.

Dr. Bernard Heuvelmans coined the term Cryptozoology, and it simply means the 'Scientific Study Of Hidden Animals'. The following breakdown is how the word was derived, and is of Greek origin: *Kruptos* meaning 'hidden', *Zoon* is 'animal', and *Logos* means 'discourse'.

ANIMALS & PESTS

NAME: Cockroach On The Tongue
CODE: AN1603
ORIGIN: Unknown
STATUS: False

Cockroach On The Tongue

In California, a lady cut her tongue while licking an envelope. At first the lady thought nothing of it, but after a week her tongue began to swell up. She went to see a doctor and he couldn't find anything wrong with her. After a few more days, her tongue had swollen up even more. Her tongue was now so sore that she had trouble eating. Her doctor sent her to hospital, and had an X-Ray taken to find the cause of the swelling. The doctors found a lump in her tongue, and decided to perform minor surgery. When her tongue was cut open, a small, live cockroach crawled out.

After investigation, they determined that the envelope seal had cockroach eggs on it. The eggs were then embedded in the cut on the tongue. The eggs were able to hatch because of the lady's saliva, and the conditions being warm and moist.

Andy Hume quoted "Hey, I used to work in an envelope factory. You wouldn't believe the things that float around in those gum applicator trays. I haven't licked an envelope for years."

Summary

This disgusting and revolting tale would make anyone think twice before licking another envelope, but the story has many flaws to its creditability. The main issue is that cockroaches do not lay their eggs in the way described. Apparently, a cockroach carries its eggs around with it in a hard capsule called an ootheca. Cockroach eggs cannot survive outside of the ootheca. This fact alone blows any creditability this UL had right out of the window!

Another question needs to be raised; who is Andy Hume? Is there such a person, and if so whom did he make the quote to? So in the words of a famous Hip Hop artist 'Will the real Andy Hume please stand up'?

Final Thoughts

Although this UL does have an oral tradition, it has spread rapidly through the use of chain E-Mails, and can feel firmly established in the cyber world of Netlore.

ANIMALS & PESTS

```
NAME:     The Log Flume Horror
CODE:     AN1604
ORIGIN:   Unknown
STATUS:   False
```

The Log Flume Horror

A young couple boarded the log flume ride at a certain theme park in Florida. It was a sweltering day, and they both felt very hot and bothered after queuing for half an hour. Just as the ride started, the girlfriend suggested that her boyfriend put his wrists in the water, her mum had always told her to run cold water over her wrists to keep cool. The boyfriend shrugged and said that he would give it a go. But as soon as he put one arm in the water, he felt a sudden pain and pulled his arm out sharply. The boy was obviously in agony, and the girlfriend called out to stop the ride but to no avail. The boyfriend complained that his arm felt like it was burning and by the time the ride had finished, the boy's arm was a horrible colour, he had fallen unconscious and was hardly breathing. He was rushed to the local hospital, but died on the way. It was quickly established that he had died from snakebites, and an investigation was immediately carried out on the log flume ride. After the log flume ride had been drained of all water, the investigators found the answer to the mystery. Near the starting point of the ride, they found a huge nest of water snakes!

Summary

The water snakes in this UL are often named as Water Moccasins (or Cottonmouths as they are also known as), the reason being that Water Moccasins are the only venomous Water Snake. Although, it is unlikely that this event ever took place as Cottonmouths do not form nests. They are solitary animals and do not live in colonies. They are not vicious, but would defend themselves violently if under threat. The venom from a Cottonmouth is not life threatening and can easily be treated. Some people have quoted that the bite is not much worse than a bee sting.

So, all these facts combined, blasts a hole through this UL big enough to drive a double decker bus through it! So why does this UL continue to survive? Its survival is dependant on the fear of snakes. Throughout time, snakes have been cast as the evil villain in the screenplay that we call life. From Adam & Eve to the Jungle Book, snakes are the spellbinding evil serpents that cunningly manipulate good intentions. They are seen as deadly predators, and can strike without warning and with great speed.

Snakes are the subject of many UL's, many similar to this version. Another popular UL involves a water skier falling into a nest of Water Moccasins, with similar fatal results. Snakes are also to be found on fair ground rides, notably the tunnel of love and the Merry-go-round. All the versions have one thing in common; the bite always results in a death.

Final Thoughts

It is almost impossible to trace the origins of this UL, although it was quite popular in some parts of the US as far back as the late1960's. This tale is one of many that fall under a certain category, a warning of dangers in so-called places of fun such as theme parks. Perhaps the reason being is that the more we enjoy ourselves, the more we relax our guard, making us more open to dangers.

ANIMALS & PESTS

```
NAME:     The Imported Snake
CODE:     AN1605
ORIGIN:   USA, 1968
STATUS:   False
```

The Snake In The Coat: Example 1

A friend of my uncle's visited a large department store to buy a new coat. She tried on about a dozen coats, and none of them suited her. She was about to give up when another coat caught her eye; she just had to try it on. As soon as she had slipped her arm into the coat, she felt a sudden and sharp piercing pain shoot up through her arm. She felt dizzy and collapsed on the floor; an ambulance was called. When the ambulance men arrived, the lady was quickly diagnosed as suffering from snakebite. An investigation took place and two small snakes were found in the arm of the last coat that the lady had tried on. The coat had been imported from Korea. The lady has since recovered and is at present suing the store.

The Snake In The Blanket: Example 2

A woman shopping at a local discount store decided to buy a blanket that had caught her eye. As she put her hand into the fold of the blanket to feel the quality and texture of the blanket, she felt a sharp prick on her hand. Her arm immediately swelled up like a balloon and turned a deep shade of red. The woman stumbled backwards and collapsed on the floor. She was rushed to hospital but unfortunately died on the way.

When the police opened the blankets up, they found a nest of baby snakes hidden inside. An investigation found that the blankets were cheap imports from China.

Summary

Born in 1968, this UL is a merger of two popular themes. The first one is the general mistrust of large retail establishments; especially budget department stores. The Americans have always been weary of anything not made in the States, and the influx of cheap imports from the Far East was seen by some as a threat to the American industries. The products are portrayed as of sub-standard quality, cheaply made and of mass production. The large retail establishments are the targets of these UL's, being blamed for poor quality control.

The second popular theme is of course finding a dangerous animal in an urban environment. In this respect, the legend shares similarities to the *Spiders In Plants* legends (AN1601), and has been linked by an American tabloid newspaper to earlier versions of the *Log Flume Horror* (AN1604).

This UL can be seen as a cautionary tale, teaching us to be aware at all times. Perhaps the message is supposed to be a blunt criticism of being 'cheap' and not buying good quality items.

Helped by heavy media coverage, the original *Snake In The Blanket* (Example 2) legend became widespread in the US during 1968 and '69. Newspapers were running reports of supposed incidents, and most people actually believed the hype. Targeted department stores had to restore confidence with their customers by making formal statements denying anything of this nature ever took place. Snakes were starting to be found in every garment imaginable, everything from rugs, rolls of carpets, blouses, jumpers and coats (as in *Example 1*). Then, strangely enough, the legend almost died a sudden death in the 1970's. As quickly as it had burst onto the scene, this UL almost disappeared in a wisp of smoke. Only clawing its way back from the brink of distinction with a vengeance. In 1991 the legend was back on the scene, only this time it was only Viper snakes in Winter Coats. The new target for the legend was a particular company (which will remain unnamed) which is famous the world over for their coats.

The victim in these legends is always a woman, and either dies from the snakebite, or recovers and sues the company involved. With the latter, normally a figure for the amount the victim is suing for is large and is usually stated. The actual breed of snake varies with different variations of the UL, but in latter versions the snake is always a Viper.

Some of the 'targeted' companies of the legend complained of foul play by rival businesses, but this has never been proved and is unlikely. To dictate rumours on this grand scale would take a huge marketing coup of the unlikeliest kind, a flawless 'smearing' campaign.

Final Thoughts

A bizarre and popular theory to the origins of the legend is the psychological link to the Vietnam War. It is believed that the legend was born in the late 1960s, with the fight against communism in Vietnam in full flight. With this in mind, the Americans had total mistrust and fear of anything connected to the Far East.

PROJECT 2067

NAME: The Dead Cat Package
CODE: AN1606
ORIGIN: At least since 1904
STATUS: False

The Dead Cat Package: Version 1

A young lady was living in a one-bedroom apartment in the heart of the West End in London. The apartment was small and the rent was extortionate, but it was close to the British Museum where she worked. Although she enjoyed the intense West End atmosphere, she still felt lonely as the cold dark evenings drew in and winter was approaching. To combat the loneliness, the young lady's solution was to buy a pet cat.

The lady loved her cat, and all was well for a couple of years, until one grey morning when she found her cat had died in its sleep. The lady had no back garden and couldn't bear to throw the body of her beloved cat in the dustbin, so she decided to bury her cat in a pet cemetery. After making a few enquiries, she found out that the nearest pet cemetery was ten miles away.

The lady decided to make the journey by tube and set about getting ready. She put the body of the cat carefully into a box and then into a large shopping bag. The lady decided to stop off at a certain clothes shop en-route, as she didn't normally travel that far and so hadn't visited this particular shop in a very long time. When in the shop, she was looking at a couple of dresses and put the large bag down for a second. When she went to pick up the bag moments later, she found that the bag was missing.

Suddenly there was a lot of commotion just outside the shop. When the lady when to see what was happening, she saw that a woman had fainted and was out cold. Clutched to her chest was the lady's carrier bag, with the head of the dead cat protruding out of the bag. The woman was a known shoplifter who had been operating in that area for months.

The Dead Cat Package: Version 2

Two old ladies were on their way to do some last minute Christmas shopping at the local shopping centre, when they accidentally ran over and killed a cat that had shot out in front of the car. The old lady who was driving was extremely distressed and couldn't leave the body of the cat on the road side, she had to give it a decent burial. So she placed the dead cat in a spare bag and put it in the car, with the intent of burying the body in her back garden after the shopping trip.

After arriving at the shopping centre and parking the car, the two old ladies decided to have a cup of tea at the café to settle their nerves. Worried about the smell of the dead cat in her car, one of the ladies placed the bag outside by the front wheel.

The café overlooked the car park, and they could clearly see the car from where they were seated. While they were drinking their cups of tea, they saw a woman casually walk up to their car and pick up the bag. The woman then walked to the café and ordered herself a coffee. The two old ladies were shocked and slightly curious to what would happen next. Sure enough, the woman slipped her hand into the bag to inspect her stolen goods, and with a loud shriek fainted and fell to the floor.

An Ambulance was called, and the woman (who was still out cold) was taken away on a stretcher. Before she was placed in the Ambulance, one of the ladies placed the bag across the woman's lap and told the Ambulance men "I think this belongs to her!"

Summary

This UL is typically morally based with the saying 'What goes around, comes around' ringing very true with this legend, the thief (and it is always a woman) always gets her just desserts for her evil deed. This UL also tackles the urban problem of disposing the bodies of dead pets when you live in the city. Most flats and apartments to not have gardens, and you cannot flush them down the toilet, but you have to dispose of the body somehow!

In both *Version 1* and *Version 2*, the dead cat is stolen by opportunitist thieves, believing the package to be recently bought goods. Proving the saying true that crime doesn't pay, the thieves get a little more than they bargained for. In other versions the package is not stolen deliberately, but simply gets mixed up with a similar package. The mix up normally takes place on a form of transport, like trains, buses and ferries. The dead cat package usually gets swapped for a package containing meat, a joint of ham for instance. In these legends, the reaction of the person who pulls out a dead cat instead of his/her dinner, is always left to the imagination!

Final Thoughts

The *Dead Cat Package* legends are certainly no spring chickens, they can be traced back almost 100 years. The earliest printed version was found in an article in the New York Times in 1904.

ANIMALS & PESTS

```
NAME:     Alligators In The Sewer
CODE:     AN1607
ORIGIN:   New York, 1930's
STATUS:   Undecided
```

Alligators In The Sewer: Example 1

Florida, with its glorious beaches and sunny climate, is a popular holiday destination for Americans. During the 1930's, New Yorkers brought back baby alligators as souvenirs from the Everglades. Within a couple of weeks the baby alligators started growing and became unmanageable as pets. Some owners dumped the alligators in the street, but the preferred method by New Yorkers was to flush them down the toilet.

The alligators thrived in the moist conditions of the sewers, feeding on sewer rats and occasionally the odd Sewer workman who was unlucky enough to stumble into their path. Because the alligators live in complete darkness and never see the sunlight, they have evolved and become albinos.

Alligators In The Sewer: Example 2

In 1935, the New York Times ran a story about how a group of boys stumbled across an alligator in the New York Sewers. One boy was shovelling snow into an open manhole down East 123rd Street, Manhattan. Suddenly, he saw something moving directly beneath him. After a closer inspection, the boy jumped to his feet and called over to his friends that he could see an alligator.

The news article carries on about how the boys managed to drag the alligator out into the open, and explains how the alligator is slain when it turns vicious. The article reports that the reptile was described as being between seven and a half and eight feet long.

Summary

The legend of the *Alligators in the Sewer* may have originated from the New York Times newspaper article explained in *Version 2*. A further discussion point to the creditability of the legend can be found in a book written by a former New York City Commissioner of Sewers. In the book he claims that by the mid 1930's, there was a problem with alligators in the sewers. The problem was treated as serious, and another commissioner headed the investigation. He claimed that they did find alligators, but they only averaged about 2 feet in length. A campaign was immediately started to rid the Manhattan sewers of the reptiles, and in 1937 it was announced that the alligators in the sewers had been exterminated.

These accounts may be plausible, but must not be taken as gospel. There may be grains of truth in the stories, but they may have been heavily exaggerated as well. Over the years the legend has grown in stature and popularity, with plausible background information on how the alligators got to be in the sewers in the first place and how they survive becoming apparent. It is true that Florida is a popular holiday destination for Americans, especially those who need to escape from the city for a while. It is also possible that baby alligators were brought back to the city as pets, as well as reptiles. But experts say it is imposible for the alligators to survive in the sewers for any great length of time. It is true that the sewer's water is a lot warmer than the rivers, but the toxic gases, hydrogen sulphide, and the industrial chemical wastes that engulf the sewers, would make the chances of survival minimal.

Another important aspect of the legend is the reproduction of the alligators over generations. This again, has more holes than Swiss cheese! Alligators nest in decaying vegetation and need the sun. The sex of the off spring depends on the temperature of the nest. If it is less than 86 degrees, then the alligators will be female. The nest needs to be over 93 degrees for the alligators to be born male. So, with the situation of the sewers, the temperature will always be less than 86 degrees, meaning none of the newborn alligators will be male. This would make it imposible for them to breed!

As the legend developed over the years, a common motif in the story was that the alligator's evolution turned them into albinos (no, they are not people from a small country near Macedonia!). It is very likely that the dark condition of the sewers would have made the alligators almost blind, and after generations would have turned albino. Perhaps they smoke too much of the white weed that is said to grow in the sewers, originating from all the marijuana that got flushed down the toilet during drug raids. But that's another story!

Final Thoughts

Perhaps these legends stem from the deep fascination and fear of what is really lurking underneath our cities. Is it really possible for such ferocious and dangerous predators to be lurking in the shadows of our cosmopolitan urban cities?

One theory is that this UL originated from an old Victorian legend about wild hogs (pigs) living in the sewers of London.

PROJECT 2067

NAME: Kaspar, The Wooden Cat
CODE: AN1608
ORIGIN: The Savoy Hotel, 1926
STATUS: True

Kaspar, The Wooden Cat

Before leaving for South Africa in 1898, the diamond king Woolf Joel held a grand dinner party at the famous Savoy Hotel in London. Unfortunately, one of his guests cancelled at the last moment, which left a party of thirteen to sit at the table. A superstitious guest mentioned that it was unlucky to dine with thirteen people at the table, but everyone else just laughed it off. The dinner party was a success, and the host said his farewells before leaving the table. Again, the guest warned him of the superstition, informing the host that whoever leaves the table first will be the first person to die. Woolf Joel, obviously not a superstitious man, found this hilarious and dismissed the idea before leaving. Within a few weeks, Woolf Joel was shot dead in his office in Johannesburg.

Fearful of any future repercussions caused by the superstition, the Savoy Hotel management provided a member of staff to sit at the table with parties of thirteen. This proved to be unpopular with guests wanting to discuss private or personal matters, and so the Hotel was forced to find another solution to the problem.

In 1926, Basil Ionides was commissioned to design a three-foot high black wooden cat, which he carved out of a single piece of London plane. The cat was named Kaspar, and is provided at parties as the fourteenth guest. Kaspar has each course served to him like any other guest of the table, even having a napkin tied around his wooden neck!

Winston Churchill was so fond of Kaspar he insisted that the wooden cat should be present at every meeting of 'The Other Club', which has always been held at the Savoy Hotel. To this day, members of 'The Other Club' have respected their founding member's wish, as Kaspar has attended every fortnightly meeting since 1927.

ANIMALS & PESTS

Summary

The superstitious fear of sitting thirteen people at the table originates from Norse Mythology. The legend tells of a banquet held in Valhalla, to which twelve Gods had been invited. The evil spirit Loki gate crashed the party and killed Balder, the favourite of the Gods. As Loki brought the total number of the party up to thirteen, it is considered an unlucky number.

Also, the number thirteen is significant to Christians because it was the total number seated at the table of the Last Supper. There was Jesus and his twelve disciples, one of which was the traitor Judas, who betrayed Jesus. Judas arrived at the table last, and so was the thirteenth member to join the party.

The story of Kaspar is an intriguing part of The Savoy Hotel's rich history. After five years work and to great expense, the Savoy Hotel opened for the first time to much speculation on the 6th August 1889. This grand hotel quickly established a reputation for elegance and style, boasting unheard of features, such as full electric lighting and the unbelievable amount of 70 baths. Over the years, the guest list reads like a 'Who's who' list of celebrities, politicians, writers, poets and the cream of high society. Lavish and extravagant parties were held at the Hotel, one of which included a baby elephant as a showpiece. The story of Woolf Joel's dinner party and his untimely death would have spread rapidly across the high society world, bringing with it new fears of the superstition. The Savoy Hotel's knee jerk reaction to seat a member of staff at every table of thirteen was probably only partly to do with the superstition, and more to do with being a damage limitations exercise to restore their reputation.

For obvious reasons, parties found a member of staff sitting at their table to be intrusive. So, in 1926, Basil Ionides was commissioned to design and create Kaspar, the black wooden cat. Basil Ionides came from a family clan of Byzantine Greeks who emigrated to England around 1820, and became the patrons of London's art world in the late 19th century. Basil had established himself as an architect and an Art Deco designer, designing many of the prestigious hotels, restaurants and theatres of the time.

So, I hear you ask, why a cat? Throughout the ages, cats have played an important role in many forms of mythology and superstition, and black cats are considered to be a lucky omen.

Final Thoughts

Winston Churchill always insisted that Kaspar was a guest of 'The Other Club', whose fortnightly meetings were held in the 'Pinafore Room' at the Savoy Hotel. Churchill jointly founded the club with F.E. Smith in 1910, with the ideal of breaking down the barriers of politics, allowing politicians from across the political span to discuss and debate issues in a friendly and relaxed manner. The party was always served with exquisite cuisine, the finest wines and they smoked quality cigars; Churchill hardly missed a meeting.

In fact, rumour has it that Churchill was so fond of Kaspar, that when two mischievous RAF personnel catnapped Kaspar and flew him to Singapore during World War Two, Churchill ordered his immediate return!

Kaspar has also had a brief appearance in the harrowing novel '48, written by James Herbert.

HORROR...

INTRODUCTION..PAGE 96

THE DEAD PROFESSOR...PAGE 98

THE MIDNIGHT SCREAM ....PAGE 100

THE LICKED HAND..PAGE 102

AIDS MARY...PAGE 104

BURIED ALIVE!...PAGE 106

FLESH FOR SALE..PAGE 108

THE HAIRY ARMED HITCHHIKER.........................PAGE 110

THE BLAIR WITCH PROJECT..................................PAGE 112

THE HALLOWEEN HORROR PREDICTION............PAGE 115

TRICKS IN TREATS...PAGE 117

PROJECT 2067

Tuesday, 16th August
12.30hrs: Just finished Brunch meeting with Max

CATEGORY: HORROR

What are you supposed to eat for Brunch? It is too late in the day to eat anything Breakfast orientated, and too early to eat lunch. It isn't a real meal, just a pretender stuck in the middle between Breakfast and Lunch. Being very indecisive, I somehow ended up with a large Pizza. What was I thinking off? Choosing something that looks like it has already been eaten and recycled by the local drunk, is not the ideal choice for a business brunch! It didn't help that I hadn't washed my hands after I had eaten, and when we got up to leave, I gave Max a handshake with a hand that felt like it had been rubbed over the head of a spotty 13 year old grease ball after an intensive P.E lesson. All in all, not a successful meeting!

So, to plan B. I am meeting Max again later after work at a bar named 'Charlie's', two blocks down from here. He is not convinced with my progress, and wants me to justify the huge hole I am eating into the company's budget. I had better do some smooth talking, or he will pull the plug on the whole project.

I need to dig deeper and look beyond the façade of UL's. I need to find out what makes them tick and the influence they have on our lives. While I keep digging (my own grave if I'm not careful!), I have gathered together some more UL's for you to study. The following section is Horror, and is a selection of legends not for the faint hearted. Some of these UL's are bordering on the '*Classic Horror*' tag, and some of you may believe that they should be classed as classic, but since this is my project and it's my hairy arse on the line, I have to make the decisions and I will stick to them!

Right, give me a moment while I climb down from my soapbox, and we will proceed. I have started the Horror section with a proto-legend from 'Down Under', meaning it is at the beginning of the Urban Legend process. Whether it will make Urban Legend status, only time will tell.

Also included are such horror/slasher favourites as '*The Hairy Armed Hitchhiker*' (HO4607), '*The Licked Hand*' (HO4603) and '*The Midnight Scream*' (HO4602). All of which gives us pure horror stripped to the bone and in its most basic form, and so survives and succeeds in their simplicity.

HORROR

On the other end of the scale we have '*The Blair Witch Project*' (HO4608), a complex but manufactured UL designed to market a product. This is a good example of how a UL can be created to manipulate and control a certain situation; in this case it was used to create hype to market a film. I feel that the use of UL's in this manner is a small hint to their potential, and something I hope to tap into and reveal later in the project.

We also explore the fear of being buried alive (HO4605), as well as looking at the illegal and sinister trade of selling human flesh for consumption in *Flesh For Sale* (HO4606). Also included are a couple of UL's from the original fright night, Halloween. At the same time every year these legends reappear on the scene, capturing the spirit of Halloween. The disturbing thing is, one of these UL's is true!

PROJECT 2067

```
NAME:     The Dead Professor
CODE:     HO4601
ORIGIN:   Australia
STATUS:   Undecided
```

The Dead Professor

A female student taking English at Adelaide University (Australia) was finishing off an assignment that had a dead line of 12 o'clock that night. By the time she had finished, she was running late and had to dash across campus in the pouring rain to hand her assignment in. The 'assignment completion box' was outside the English Department on the 6th floor of a building called the Napier Block. By the time she had reached the Napier Block, the girl was completely soaked to the skin.

While the girl was waiting for the lift to take her up to the 6th floor, she felt increasingly uneasy. The building seemed empty, even the cleaners had gone home. The building was in complete darkness, as no lights had been left on. Although the girl knew that this was not unusual considering what time of night it was, she still couldn't help getting a little spooked.

When the student got out of the lift on the 6th floor, she failed to notice that a light was on in a room at the end of the corridor, about seven rooms away from where the assignment completion box was situated.

After handing in her assignment, the student pressed the button to call the lift. By the time the lift had come, she was shivering from the cold and just wanted to go to bed. Just as the lift doors opened, a professor came out of the room at the end of the corridor and turned the lights out. When he saw the lift doors open, he ran down the corridor to catch the lift. The student saw him coming, and feeling scared, quickly closed the lifts doors shouting out "Sorry you will have to take the next one". She knew it was silly, but the girl felt very vulnerable and uneasy about the whole situation. As the doors closed, the professor looked very shocked and distressed. The student felt very guilty but put this out of her mind as she ran back across campus.

The next day, the student went back to the Napier block to apologise to the professor and explain the situation, but found his door still locked. When she went to the English department and asked where he was, they explained that he had died of a heart attack during the night. Apparently the heart attack was not a major one, but he had been unable to press the button to call the lift as he had collapsed on the floor. By the time he had been found by the cleaners in the morning, he was already dead.

It is said that when you wait for the lifts in the Napier Block late at night, they will always take you to the 6th floor. Also, if you look in the mirrors at the back of the lifts when the doors close, you will see the horrified and shocked face of the dead professor.

It is also rumoured that if look at the Napier Block on a rainy night, at exactly 12 o'clock, the lights in the end room of the 6th floor flash on and off several times as the ghost of the professor vents out his anger.

Summary

This simple ghost story is what I would class as a 'Proto-legend', which basically means an Urban Legend in the making. Whether this story will make it to the status of UL only time will tell, perhaps I have helped it on its way by re-telling the story here!

I am unclear of the origins of this legend, as I have only spotted it a couple of times on the Internet, both times written anonymously. I have E-Mailed Adelaide University three or four times asking them if they could cast any light on the subject, but either the legend is shrouded in secrecy or the University is not one for correspondence as I have had no replies to date. In one of the versions I read, it described the story as a local Adelaide legend. With this in mind, I have tried to contact various organisations within the Adelaide community, again with no results. It seems that no one wants to talk about this ghost story, how mysterious!

Final Thoughts

The Dead Professor is a typical campus horror story, similar to thousands of other legends told by students in Universities across the world. Each University will own at least one legend that gets told across the campus year after year. This legend may have gone no further than the Adelaide University campus. If it has, I doubt if it has spread any further than the local Adelaide community.

Whatever the origins, this is simply a good old fashioned classic ghost story.

PROJECT 2067

```
NAME:     The Midnight Scream
CODE:     HO4602
ORIGIN:   USA
STATUS:   False
```

The Midnight Scream

In colleges across America, they used to have a rule of silence for a designated week to help students study for their exams. During these weeks in the 1960's a new craze was born called the Midnight Scream. At the stroke of midnight on a designated day, all the students at every college would lean out their windows or rush outside, and scream their heads off for five minutes solid. This was said to have been a great stress relief!

During one particular Midnight Scream, a young female student was running down the fire exit staircase to join her friends outside for the traditional scream, when all of a sudden she was grabbed from behind. Her attacker dragged her down the remaining stairs and into a dark corner, all the time the girl was screaming for help. Of course, her cries were in vain and lost in all the commotion. The next morning, the girl's mutilated body was found at the bottom of the stairwell.

Since then, every college in America has banned the Midnight Scream from taking place.

Summary

The strange custom of the Midnight Scream (also known as 'Primal Screams' or 'Door Slams') actually does take place by students at college in the USA. The screaming or slamming of doors is considered a great stress relief, as the students are under enormous pressure preparing for their final exams. The period of silence that is commonly known as the 'dead period' takes place just before the exams and is designed to help the students concentrate with their studies. In reality the 'dead period' can be anything from a day to a week long.

So far, so good, but at this point reality signs out and fiction clocks in! To the best of my knowledge and research, an incident like this has never happened. In some versions of this UL, the girl is raped and not murdered, but again, this is fiction and not reality. This legend, like so many others, was probably born out of the insecurity felt by students, caused by living away from home.

Final Thoughts

Although this Legend can be classed as fiction, it may have roots in similar real life cases. There have been many incidents where someone has been attacked and their cries for help have been ignored. Sometimes this is because of the 'Crying Wolf' syndrome, because people in some areas hear screaming quite often (most of the time caused by kids mucking around), they fail to detect and react to a real situation. The other, and unfortunately disturbing reason, is that some people are too self absorbed with their own existence to care about the welfare of anyone else.

PROJECT 2067

```
NAME:     The Licked Hand
CODE:     HO4603
ORIGIN:   Unknown
STATUS:   False
```

The Licked Hand

A young girl was left at home one night while her parents went out for a meal. As instructed, the girl went around the house closing and locking all the windows. She managed to lock every single window but for one, which was in the basement. She decided that would have to do, as she wasn't tall enough to reach the window.

After having a shower and watching TV, the young girl decided to go to bed. Feeling a little uneasy about being in the house alone, she took her pet dog into the bedroom with her. As usual, the dog positioned it self under the bed, and the girl let her hand hang over the edge of the bed so the dog could lick her hand. She found this comforting and soon fell asleep.

Shortly into the night, the girl awoke to the sound of dripping from the bathroom. She was absolutely sure that she had turned the shower off properly before, and felt too scared to get out of bed. So she hanged her arm over the bed for her dog to lick her hand, and promptly fell back asleep.

The approaching headlights of her parent's car woke the girl again a few hours later. Still hearing the dripping noise, she decided to go to the bathroom and make sure the shower was turned off properly. As soon as the girl opened the bathroom door, she froze in terror. Hanging by its collar over the shower curtain rail, swung the mutilated cut body of her dog.

The girl rushed back to her room in panic, and looked under the bed to where her dog had been licking her hand. She found a note that had been written in neat handwriting simply saying 'Humans can lick too, my dear!'

```
Summary
```

A version of this legend was printed in a book as part of a collection of modern fairy tales called 'One Potato, Two Potato' by Mary & Herbert Knapp, in 1976. The version above closely resembles the one printed in that book, although there are many variants to this UL. In one version, there are two girls in the house alone. The ending is particularly gruesome as one of the girls kops it, along with her four legged friend.

The gruesome ending for the dog is a common motif in all versions of this legend, and the message left at the scene appears in most versions. Sometimes the message is written in the blood of the dog on the floor, and sometimes is worded "Humans can lick too, you know!"

In one version a slight twist is added with the story being staged at a girls slumber party. The girl who is holding the slumber party is extremely snobbish, and refuses to sleep in the same room as the other girls. She instead sleeps in her own bedroom with her pet dog. The story then follows on with the same formula as all the other versions, except all her guests are slaughtered as well (and I don't mean drunk!)

The Licked Hand runs the same formula as many other Horror legends, most of them you will find in the *Classic Horror* section. I was in two minds whether or not to include this legend with the classics. Although the popularity of this UL is growing, it has not reached such a cult status as some of the other horror legends from the same generation. I am sure many of you disagree, but it is a free world isn't it? The formula I speak of is the same formula used in slasher/horror films, the tales are normally gruesome and straight to the point. The intent is to make an immediate impact, using a chilling mixture of pure horror, revulsion and fear. Like with so many other legends, this may have arisen as a cautionary tale aimed at children. Perhaps the tale actually originated from the children, harbouring their deep inner fear of being left alone at night.

Final Thoughts

This UL shares great similarities with *The Roommates Death* (HR4706), especially with the chilling message left at the scene by the intruder. In both UL's, the crime takes place right under the nose of the unsuspecting subjects, and this violation is brought into clarity by the mocking but chilling message.

PROJECT 2067

```
NAME:      AIDS Mary
CODE:      HO4604
ORIGIN:    1986
STATUS:    False
```

AIDS Mary

A bloke and his mates went out clubbing in Brighton for his 21st birthday. They were all having a good time and by the end of the night were all very drunk. When they all left the nightclub, the mates sprung a surprise on the birthday boy; they had arranged a hotel room and a prostitute for him for the night.

Very grateful, the birthday boy staggered to the hotel and up to his room, where he met the prostitute, who was an extremely attractive young woman. After having a good time, he fell into a deep drunken sleep. This bloke slept so soundly, he didn't wake up till 11 o'clock the next morning. With a pulsing headache, he rolled over and realised the prostitute had already got up and left.

Still suffering from a hang over and rubbing his head, the bloke staggered into the bathroom, and froze solid by what he saw. Written neatly in red lipstick across the bathroom mirror, were the words 'WELCOME TO THE WORLD OF AIDS!'

Summary

This is obviously a cautionary tale and was first circulated during the AIDS frenzy and paranoia of 1986. As public awareness grew of the deadly disease during the 1980's, so did the paranoia on a larger scale. We have already covered these fears and anxieties of the disease in *Infected Needles* (CR1707). This is an urban legend warning of the dangers of indiscriminate sex and multiple sexual partners. The age of *free sex* that started in the swinging sixties was well and truly over. No longer could people have conscience-free, unprotected sex with just about anyone they wanted, they now had to think about the consequences.

This legend also tackles issues such as the danger and immorality of sleeping with prostitutes. The 'lady of the night' in this legend obviously holds a grudge against men as a whole, which she blames for her contracting the AIDS virus.

HORROR

She is seeking revenge without discrimination, and this poor unsuspecting bloke is the latest hapless victim.

Similar real life occurrences have occurred over the years. A British woman actually did contract the disease from her Greek lover while in Greece. The man, knowing he was HIV positive, had sexual intercourse with the woman without informing her of his condition. In America, there have been cases of multiple amounts of people being infected by one person through sexual intercourse. Although it is not normally possible to prove if malice was involved, there has been at least one person (Pamela Wiser, Tennessee, USA) who has been convicted of this crime.

Final Thoughts

Another popular urban legend that is closely related to this one is *AIDS Harry*. This is a tale of similar motifs, but the perpetrator is male. The legend normally tells of a holiday romance in a country such as Greece. When the girl returns home, her male lover gives her a present; a souvenir of their romance. When the lady opens the present, it is always something like a mug, with the words 'Welcome to the world of AIDS!' written on it.

PROJECT 2067

NAME: **Buried Alive!**
CODE: HO4605
ORIGIN: Unknown
STATUS: Undecided

Buried Alive!

The old man had loved his wife and they had been married for over 50 years. So when she died, he was absolutely devastated. In fact, he was positive she was still alive and had to be dragged away from her body when the doctor pronounced her dead.

In years gone by, the deceased body would not have been drained of any body fluids, and would have simply been placed in the coffin. It was also common for poor folk to have a burial plot in their back garden, as in this case. The old man still insisted his wife was not dead, and told the doctor that he knew his wife was still alive because he could still feel her presence. At which point the old man became hysterical and had to be heavily sedated before being put to bed while his wife was being buried.

That night the old man awoke with a vision so vividly horrific, he couldn't stop screaming. The doctor was called, and the old man told him that in his vision his wife was still alive and was frantically clawing at the inside of the coffin. The old man was so certain of his vision; the doctor decided that they would have to dig up the coffin just to put his mind at rest.

The next morning, the coffin was dug up and opened. When they opened the lid, they were met by a sight that would make your blood run cold. The old lady's face was distorted into an eternal scream, and her hands facing upwards with the finger nails completely bent back. Scratch marks were clearly visible on the inside of the coffin lid. The poor woman had been buried alive!

Summary

The origin of this UL is unknown, but it is very likely that the legend originated from the paranoid fears that engulfed the 18th and 19th centuries of being buried alive. This common fear coincided with major breakthroughs in medical practices and techniques; one of these was the technique of resuscitation. People, who would have been presumed dead before, could now be brought back to life. The thought of being declared dead when you are still alive plagued the minds of many. The realisation that many people had been buried alive didn't help much either! Many of the coffins that had been dug up (normally by grave robbers) were found to have scratch marks or other disturbances inside. In those days, this was taken as proof of being buried alive, we know now of other explanations for this strange occurrence.

In those days, bodies were not embalmed before they were buried, and the bodies were placed into coffins soon after their death. It is believed that the contractions of muscles, could move the body into different positions, this could cause the scratch marks on the inside of the coffin. Another explanation is the gas pressure inside the bodies; this could also cause the strange events seen inside the coffins.

Final Thoughts

In the 18th and 19th centuries, the fear of being buried alive was so great that signalling devices for the coffins were common practice. These included placing a bell on top of the grave, with a pull rope run down into the coffin. Small flags or electric lights were also activated in this manner.

PROJECT 2067

```
NAME:      Flesh For Sale
CODE:      HO4606
ORIGIN:    Unknown
STATUS:    Undecided
```

Flesh For Sale

The after effects of World War 2 plunged Germany into recession. During this time of desperation, money and food was short. At the same time, a strange tale was being spread by word of mouth through the streets of Berlin. It was said that a young woman had met and got chatting to a blind man at a rally, and at some point during the conversation he had asked her for a favour. The blind man wanted the young woman to deliver a letter to the house of a friend of his. The woman agreed, and took down the address of the house. She had become suspicious when after crossing the street; she had looked back over her shoulder to observe the blind man scurrying away into the crowds without the aide of his stick. Instead of delivering the letter, the woman went straight to the police.

The police raided the address that the letter was supposed to have been delivered to, and found heaps of human flesh that was ready for sale. After opening the letter, they found a note that read 'This is the last one I am sending you today'.

Summary

I have not been able to prove if this elaborate tale is authentic, but what I have found out is that it could be based on elements of truth. The legend has a backdrop of post war Berlin; Germany had just lost the war and the country was in turmoil. During these times work was scarce, and money even scarcer. It is possible that certain people would resort to cannibalism, and even capitalise on the situation by selling human flesh just to stay alive. It is also possible that this legend mutated from a piece of Nazi propaganda. During the war, rumours of Polish Jews killing young German girls for food were rife in Germany. Of course there has been no evidence of such atrocities.

There is, however, enough evidence to suggest that the sinister trade of selling human flesh and organs does exist. One report I read was investigating life after communism in the poverty stricken ex-soviet countries. There was one documented case from the Republic of Moldova, where a cleaner stole body parts that were ready for incineration and sold them to two local women. The woman then cut up the body parts into steak sized portions and sold them on the streets, selling them for half the usual price for meat of that size. One customer was suspicious, and the tests that followed proved that the meat was human. The Health Ministry launched an investigation.

Acts out of desperation and hunger of this kind have also been reported in other suppressed and poverty stricken countries. It is claimed that in North Korea, human flesh can be bought openly at a farmer's market. Apparently, another disturbing claim is that orphans are sold on the black market with the intent to be used as food. Although there are many dying of starvation in this communist state, the farmers have been ordered to stop growing food, and to grow opium instead. The opium is processed into heroin, and sold into the illegal drug trade abroad.

Final Thoughts

A piece of netlore has spread around the web lately in the form of a disturbing E-Mail. The E-Mail states that Web site *Manbeef.com* are marketing human flesh for human consumption. To protest, you put your name on the petition at the bottom of the E-Mail and send it on.

Believe it or not, there is a Web site called *Manbeef.com*, and they have marketed gourmet cuts of butchered human meat. But reportedly this was done as a hoax, and was only intended to be a joke!

PROJECT 2067

```
NAME:    The Hairy Armed Hitchhiker
CODE:    HO4607
ORIGIN:  At least since 1836
STATUS:  Unknown
```

The Hairy Armed Hitchhiker

As a woman was returning home in her car from a shopping trip, she noticed an old lady by the side of the road trying to thumb a lift, and obviously struggling with her shopping bag. Feeling pity for the old lady, the woman stopped and asked her if she would like a lift. The old lady gratefully accepted, and climbed into the car.

As the old lady got into the car, the young woman noticed that her passenger had large hairy wrists and arms, and was wearing a big chunky watch. Realising immediately that the old lady was in fact a man, the woman asked the 'old lady' to check if the rear lights are working. As soon as the 'old lady' got out of the car, the woman quickly drove off and headed straight for the police station. When the police examined the bag that the 'old lady' had left behind, they discovered a sharp blood, stained axe.

Summary

This variant of the *Hairy Armed Hitchhiker* is typically British, and was popular in the late 1970's. The actual legend though, goes back a lot further than that. The earliest variant found of this legend was printed in 1834 (The Stanford Mercury), and another variation appeared in a book in 1956, titled 'Negro Folktales In Michigan'.

In a modern time where hitchhiking has declined, and no longer is seen as safe or socially acceptable, the UL has had to adapt. The popularity of the legend has crossed over the big pond to the States, with the modern versions based in a Shopping Mall car park. The variations and locations of the Mall differ, but usually a woman returns to her car from a shopping trip to find an old lady sitting in the back. The old lady apologies and explains that she was tired and just wanted a rest. The woman feels pity for the old lady until she notices her hairy arms; the rest you know. The only thing that niggles me about this variation is how the old lady got into the car in the first place, surely most people lock their doors!

Another interesting point is the rise in popularity of using shopping malls as the location and back drop of modern UL's. This trend is firmly rooted in the US, where shopping malls have become the focal point of the American society. Not only are they a place for shopping, but also for meeting and socialising. Perhaps such legends as this one and *The Slasher Under The Car* (CR1705) harbour deep anxieties that something sinister could be bubbling under the surface of normality, and the shopping mall, considered by many as the safe havens of society, is no exception.

With this UL, as with so many others, the horror is what could have been and not what actually happened. We are given the tools, and it is our own imagination that is left to do the work. The perpetrator is disguised, and it is implied that the victim would be helpless. We are also told that the axe that was found was blood stained, so it is obvious that the woman wouldn't have been the first victim. The nature of the weapon, an axe, mentally visualises a particularly gruesome end for the victim was in store.

Final Thoughts

Another variant of this UL, also set in a shopping mall car park, has a man offering help to a woman with a flat tyre. After the tyre had been changed, the helpful man asked if he could just have a lift to where his car was on the other side of the car park. The woman feeling obliged because of his help, agreed. As soon as the man got into her car, the woman felt very uneasy and made an excuse about forgetting a shopping bag, hurried into the shopping mall and called security. When the security man went out to the car, the helpful man was nowhere in sight. He checked the car and found a bag in the boot that contained a hunting knife and some rope. The man must have placed the bag in there when he was changing the tyre. Another twist to the story is that the flat tyre was perfectly OK; somebody had let the air out of the tyre!

This variant is interesting because it avoids the main motif of the UL. Instead of using a disguise, the man lures his victim into a trap by setting up a clever scenario.

PROJECT 2067

```
NAME:     The Blair Witch Project
CODE:     HO4608
ORIGIN:   1999
STATUS:   False
```

The Blair Witch Project

In February 1785, a woman named Elly Kedward was accused of luring children into her home and drawing blood from them. Kedward was found guilty of witchcraft and banished from the village of Blair, Maryland. By the time of winter 1786, all of Kedward's accusers, along with half of Blair's children had vanished. Fearing a curse is upon them, the folk of Blair decide to flee.

In November 1809, a very rare book entitled 'The Blair Witch Cult' is published. Classified by many as fiction, the book describes how an outcast witch was tortured before her trial and goes on to curse the whole village. The book has seen better days, and only parts of the book can still be read.

In 1824, the town of Burkittsville was founded on the Blair site. With a population of 194, it was located in Frederick County, Maryland, and was approximately one hour from Washington DC.

During the years that followed, many strange and weird occurrences happened in and around the town of Burkittsville, with child murders and mutilations commonplace. In 1941, a man living in the town was convicted and hanged of murdering and disembowelling seven children in a ritual like manner. He claimed that it was at the behest of a ghost of an old woman who occupied the woods near his house.

In 1994, three student filmmakers ascended of the town of Burkittsville to carry out a class project studying the legend of the Blair Witch. After interviewing the locals, they disappear into the woods never to be seen again.

A massive manhunt is carried out to try and find the students, employing dogs, helicopters and a hundred men. A fly over by a department of defence satellite was even used! Ten days and 33,000 man-hours later, the search was called off. In fact, no trace was found of them until the footage they shot was discovered under an old log cabin a year later.

Summary

The Blair Witch Project was ground breaking, as it was the first time that a UL was created with the sole purpose to market a film. This low budget production used the power of UL's with maximum effect, and in doing so, achieved massive publicity before the film was even released. The Blair Witch website supplies a formidable and extremely detailed history of the legend, giving a creditable background to the film. The film itself is stated as being the actual footage filmed by the students, shortly before they disappeared. The footage was found a year after their disappearance in an abandoned log cabin, and was titled *'The Blair Witch Project'.* The whole set up was very believable, and instantly gave the film a cult status before it was even released! Of course, we all know now that the whole legend is an elaborate piece of fiction, a clever piece of marketing that was the brainchild of the film's writer/directors, Daniel Myrick and Eduardo Sanchez. Without a big budget to spend on advertising, they utilised the Internet to spin a unique piece of netlore; and it worked!

The film itself was produced in a unique way, and a selection of unknown actors were used to play the characters. The actors were told of the role of the characters they were portraying and the outline of the film, and then were dumped in the middle of the woods not knowing what was going to happen. Notes and supplies were left in strategic positions for them, and they were monitored by a Global Positioning System that helped keep track of where they were. The end result was unique film footage that has a home video documentary feel to it, where the emotions of true fear and horror can be seen quite clearly on the young actor's faces.

In truth, the film never actually lived up to the hype, although it did prove to be a popular topic for discussion after it was released due to the fact that public opinion was so vigorously divided. The infamous shaky camcorder footage has not proved to be everyone's 'cup of tea', but is essential to get that student home video feel that the film relies on.

Final Thoughts

The *Blair Witch Project* reportedly took a total of $240.5 million at the box office, and $140.5 million of that was from the US alone. To put these figures into true perspective, you have to understand that the film was made with hardly any budget.

PROJECT 2067

The *Blair Witch Project* was one of the great successes of 1999, rated at 14th position for that year's top grossing films. It even beat off big budget blockbusters, with films such as *Wild Wild West*, *American Pie*, *End Of Days*, *Entrapment* and *Big Daddy* all finishing in lower positions.

HORROR

```
NAME:    The Halloween Horror Prediction
CODE:    HO4609
ORIGIN:  At least since 1968, USA
STATUS:  False
```

The Halloween Horror Prediction

A famous psychic on a top US television talk show has predicted that a mass murder is going to take place at a college campus this Halloween. The prediction is that the murders will take place in a city that begins with the letter 'W', and at a dormitory that is 'H' shaped. The dormitory is also situated near water, probably a small lake. The number of victims will be ten, and they will all be female students. The killer will be wearing a scream mask, and the murder weapon is a hatchet.

Summary

The TV talk show that the psychic is have supposedly have appeared on is normally stated, and usually is one hosted by Oprah Winfrey or Montel Williams. The fact that no one has ever seen this particular show is sometimes explained by stating that the show was taped but never aired.

In the latest versions, the killer is said to be wearing a scream mask. In the earlier versions (pre 1998), the killer was said to be dressed up as little Bo Peep. The weapon of choice varies from version to version, but is usually a sharp instrument like a knife, hatchet or axe. The number of victims also varies, but is usually one of the following numbers; 9, 10, 12, 15 or 18.

The location of the campus is normally explained in a cryptic prediction. For instance, the campus is in a city that begins with the letter 'M' or 'W', and is adjacent to a cemetery, rail track, etc.

The *'Halloween Predictions'* rumours are very similar to other campus legends, such as *'The Midnight Scream'* (HO4602) and *'The Roommates Death'* (HR4706), and has the same psychological traits of insecurity about dormitory life on campus. This is explained in greater detail in the *Final Thoughts* of *'The College Letter'* (CM1602).

Although the rumours seem highly implausible, the threat was seen as serious enough at some universities for them to ban Little Bo Peep costumes at their Halloween parties.

Final Thoughts

This UL has been around since at least 1968, where similar rumours were abound in the eastern and midwestern universities of the US. It was said that Jean Dixon had predicted the murders on a radio programme.

The legend has had spurts of popularity in the following years; 1968, '79, '83, '86, '88, '91 and '98. The outbreak in popularity of the UL in 1998 has been heavily associated with the popular film 'Urban Legends', which had been released that same year in the cinema.

HORROR

```
NAME:     Tricks In Treats
CODE:     HO4610
ORIGIN:   USA
STATUS:   True
```

Tricks In Treats

WARNING!

Every year at Halloween, kids dress up in ghoulish costumes and go 'trick-or-treating'. This is seen as harmless fun by many and is usually carried out under adult supervision. The reason why this exercise is called 'trick-or-treat' is simple, the kids knock on a door, when a person answers they are given a simple question, trick or treat? The person then has to give the 'trick-or-treaters' a treat (e.g. sweets, chocolate, apples, etc.), or pay the penalty with a trick. The trick is usually a practical joke with no malice involved, although some kids may take this a bit too far.

This custom has been carried out for generations, and so it is a sign of the times when parents have to be vigilant and careful about the treats the kids are receiving. I am afraid there are some truly wicked and twisted people out there, whom seem to take great pleasure in tampering with the kid's treats. In some of the most serious cases, razorblades and pins have been found embedded in apples. It is only a matter of time before serious injury is caused by such mindless and callous acts.

So, I ask all parents to be extremely vigilant and not allow your children to go trick-or-treating without adult supervision. Always check the treats for signs of tampering, and especially be wary of anything homemade (e.g. cakes).

Happy trick-or-treating!

Summary

It seems unbelievable but it's true, these sick and twisted individuals that tamper with the kids treats really do exist! The warning above is typical of many that appear in E-Mail in-trays or received through fax machines just before Halloween every year. It is a warning with basis, and should never go unheeded. Over the years there has been many incidents of this kind of food tampering, and the threat has prompted official warnings to be issued. In 1997, the CPSC (Consumer Product Safety Commission) issued the following safety tip for Halloween trick-or-treating: 'Warn children not to eat any treats before an adult has examined them carefully for evidence of tampering'.

Although still a threat, the stories have turned into legends over the years and are often greatly exaggerated. Most cases reported have turned out to be hoaxes and out of the incidents that have actually happened, luckily no one has been seriously injured. The stories started to fly around in the late sixties, and the number of incidents reached a record high in 1982. In this particular year, there was an influx of food tampering instances, and not just over the period of Halloween.

Although hugely popular in the US, trick-or-treating in Britain was almost unheard of before the 1980's. When the US custom did take off in Britain in the mid 1980's, so did all the legends that went with it. British parents were particularly cautious of their kids going trick-or-treating, hearing stories about food tampering, poisoning, and kidnapping. Many households banned trick-or-treating, and trick-or-treaters were shown hostility. Of course, the media gave more than a helping hand to whip up the frenzy.

Final Thoughts

The modern practice of trick-or-treating probably originated from a Celtic New Year tradition of placing treats on the doorstep for the spirits that haunted the night, looking for people to possess. The idea was that the treats would please the spirits, and so would leave the occupants of the house in peace.

The Christians also had a similar ritual called 'souling', which would take place on the 2nd November around the 9th century AD. A participant would walk around knocking on doors, the person that answered the door would exchange 'soul cakes' (square pieces of bread with currants) for a prayer for deceased relatives. The more cakes that were given, the more prayers would be said, increasing the chances that the deceased relative's soul would find heaven.

TRAINS, PLANES, & AUTOMOBILES...

INTRODUCTION..PAGE 120

MOBILE PHONES AT PETROL STATIONS.........PAGE 123

GHOSTLY HANDPRINTS.....................................PAGE 125

THE CHICKEN GUN...PAGE 127

THE ROAD HOG..PAGE 129

BATTLE OF THE AGES......................................PAGE 131

MR.GAY..PAGE 133

THE LOCKED OUT PILOT.................................PAGE 135

THE DEATH CAR..PAGE 137

THE BEDBUG LETTER......................................PAGE 139

LIFE IS CHEAP...PAGE 141

THE JATO ROCKET CAR...................................PAGE 143

THE CLEVER MOTORIST..................................PAGE 145

THE WOODEN AIRFIELD..................................PAGE 147

PROJECT 2067

Tuesday, 16th August
23.45hrs: Arrived back at Apartment after being to Charlie's Bar

CATEGORY: TRAINS, PLANES, & AUTOMOBILES

Disaster! Going to Charlie's Bar was the worst decision I could have made. The night was a complete shambles, and I have got as much chance of carrying on with the project as Eminem has with winning the Nobel Peace Prize. The total lack of a woman's presence in the bar should have rung a few alarm bells larger than Big Ben, but it took a very hairy and extremely well tattooed biker pinching my boss's arse for the realisation to dawn that Charlie's was in fact a gay bar. Not that I have anything against gay bars, but I do prefer the sweet scent of a shapely six foot blonde girl, than the stench of a hairy biker whose religion must forbid him to wash, and whose beer belly could easily be a concealed basket ball under his dirty T-shirt.

To make matters worse, Max and I had barely started talking business when a Karaoke competition kicked in. I hate Karaoke! If I wanted to listen to a bunch of untalented drunks that do not posses a musical bone in their body, churning out a gut-wrenching version of "It's Raining Men" or "I Will Survive", I would watch a re-run of Pop Idols.

It got worse, much worse. Max got up to buy the next round of drinks when he was suddenly grabbed by his newfound friend (the hairy biker), and pulled up onto the stage with all his mates. A microphone was then shoved into Max's hand and a cowboy hat was placed onto his head. The first few bars of a song that I immediately recognised as YMCA blared out, the whole bar jumped to their feet and started cheering. Not only was Max forced to sing the song, he had to perform all the dance actions as well. Max danced liked he had ants in his pants; it was so hilarious I fell off my stool laughing. At the end of the song, the red faced Max left the stage to a standing ovation and a few catcalls and wolf whistles from the crowd. Max came straight over to our table, told me he didn't feel that well and had to leave and stormed out of the bar as fast as his chubby little legs could carry him, leaving me to wonder if my career had just disappeared with him! I guess I will just have to wait and see, but one thing is for sure, I will never see the song YMCA in quite the same light again. Moving on…

Mankind has never quite grasped the concept of adapting to the environment; it is more of the case of adapting the environment to suit mankind. Never being satisfied with just our own two feet, we have always contrived different ways to

TRAINS, PLANES, & AUTOMOBILES

help us get from A to B that little bit faster. From the invention of the wheel it has been an epic journey of discovery that can only be described as an obsession. The last century saw technology finally keeping up with our dreams, and the limits of travel suddenly seemed boundless. From flying across the Atlantic, exploring space, reaching the deepest depths of our oceans, to flying supersonic, the boundaries were pushed back further and further.

Out of all the modes of transport that we have in the modern world, the motorcar has been the one that has affected us the most. We simply could not live without them and cannot imagine what life was like before them (although I am sure people like Ken Livingstone would like to see people being flogged in the town square for driving a car in London)! Although most of us will not go as far as one particular American from one of those sunny states down south, who was so fanatical about his car, that he actually married it! It is safe to say that we are a nation that is obsessed with cars. The back category of UL's about cars is huge, and they range from the cheeky *'The Clever Motorist'* (TR8712), to the sinister *'Ghostly Handprints'* (TR8702), to the damn right stupid *'The JATO Rocket Car'* (TR8711). Just for good measures we also touch on the present day's hysteria of road rage with *'Battle Of The Ages'* (TR8705) and *'The Road Hog'* (TR8704), while discussing the reasons why you are not allowed to use mobile phones at petrol stations in *'Mobile Phones At Petrol Stations'* (TR8701).

Another obsession of mankind since year dot is the fantasy of flying. The Wright brothers gave us that dream, and it has been realised on a grand scale with commercial air travel. The airline industry is very demanding and cut throat, but also close knit, with many UL's forming from 'in-house' jokes such as *'Mr. Gay'* (TR8706) and *'The Locked Out Pilot'* (TR8707). Another legend *'The Wooden Airfield'* (TR8714) is a great example of wartime propaganda, and is what I consider as a breakthrough with Project 2067. We are now starting to see how UL's can be skilfully manipulated to serve a certain purpose.

We are not a nation that likes to complain, in most situations we are more likely to grin and bare it, keep the stiff upper lip and all that. But sometimes when certain standards are not met we feel it necessary to put pen to paper and write a letter of complaint. Normally you would receive a very apologetic letter back in return, which is known in the trade as a duck letter. Everything is fine, you have made your point and they stand corrected…unless the true feelings of the company are accidentally discovered as in the *Bedbug Letter* (TR8709).

PROJECT 2067

Finally, I would like to draw your attention to *Life Is Cheap* (TR8710). This is a gritty story that tackles issues such as the belief that there is a decline in morality in this world, and with escalating violence and death all too common in certain countries, Life really is that cheap!

TRAINS, PLANES, & AUTOMOBILES

```
NAME:     Mobile Phones At Petrol Stations
CODE:     TR8701
ORIGIN:   Unknown
STATUS:   False
```

Mobile Phones At Petrol Stations

The following is a typical warning notice circulated by E-Mail:

WARNING – DO NOT USE MOBILE PHONES AT PETROL STATIONS

A driver has suffered serious burns and his car severely damaged, when his mobile phone caused an explosion after petrol fumes ignited. He was using his mobile phone while filling his car up, when the explosion happened. All Electronic equipment at Petrol Stations are fitted with explosive containment devices for safety measures, but of course, Mobile Phones are not.

Please read your HANDBOOK carefully, as all mobile manufacturers stress caution about using mobile phones at Petrol Stations.

Summary

Although I have stated this UL as being *False*, Mobile Phones are considered a health risk at Petrol Stations. There has never been an explosion caused by the use of a Mobile Phone at a Petrol Station to date, and an explosion cannot be caused by the radio signals transmitted by mobiles igniting petrol fumes. The actual risk is if the battery of the phone drops onto the forecourt, the battery contacts may momentarily short, creating a spark that could ignite flammable vapours. This risk is not only assessed with Mobile Phones, but also with other electronic equipment that are battery operated, such as walkmans and torches.

Although the chance of this actually happening is about as likely as Bolton winning the Premiership, the threat is taken very seriously. In Great Britain, Mobile Phones are not allowed on petrol forecourts under the conditions of the Petroleum Consultation Act 1928. The person with the phone cannot be held responsible; all responsibility rests with the forecourt owner. You can now see why Petrol Stations are so strict with the use of Mobile Phones on their forecourts!

Final Thoughts

These 'warning E-Mails' exploded onto the scene in 1999, and normally referred to an incident that was supposed to have happened in Indonesia, and more recently, Australia. Investigations have found all these reports to be unfounded, and an explosion at a Petrol Station in Australia was not caused by the use of a Mobile Phone as many believe, but by static igniting petrol vapours inside a tanker after it had finished refuelling an underground diesel tank.

The *Bangkok Post* printed an article about an incident of this type happening in Indonesia, which the *China Post* reportedly originally covered. It is speculated that these articles were prompted by the chain E-Mails, and not the other way around!

TRAINS, PLANES, & AUTOMOBILES

```
NAME:      Ghostly Handprints
CODE:      TR8702
ORIGIN:    Early 1970's, USA
STATUS:    False
```

Ghostly Handprints

A few years back in a small town in America, a tragic accident happened. A school bus packed with children stalled while travelling over a railway crossing, with a train heading towards them at great speed. There was no time to evacuate the bus, and the train was travelling so fast it couldn't stop in time. Every child on that bus perished in that fatal accident.

Locally, rumours were abounding that the railway crossing was haunted, and a couple of teenagers thought that they would check this rumour out for themselves. They drove to the railway crossing and parked up right over the tracks. After a few minutes, the strangest of things happened, the car started to roll forwards of its own accord. The car continued to roll until it was completely clear of the tracks.

The teenagers jumped out of the car and rushed around to the back of it to see who was pushing it. Of course nobody was there, but they saw something that made them shudder to the bone. The car was extremely dirty and dusty from the drive out there, and all the way along the back of the car they could see little handprints in the dust, so small they could only have been made by children.

Summary

The 'Ghostly Hands' has all the hallmarks of a classic ghost legend such as 'The Vanishing Hitchhiker' (HR4704), but is thought to have originated as late as the early 1970's. The legend is told in a subtle manner, and it is left for your own imagination to fill in the gaps. We are led to believe that the spirits of the deceased school children pushed the teenagers car off the tracks and out of harms way, desperately trying to avoid another tragedy.

There are variants of this legend, but the handprints are a distinct motif in all of them. In one version it is set in the early morning, and the handprints appear in the dew. In another version, the handprints are only seen when the back of the car is inspected using a forensic technique with white powder.

Final Thoughts

Ghostly Hands is similar in many ways to the legend of *Gravity Hill*, in Scotland County (USA). Apparantly, if you stop your car at a certain place on the hill and slip the gear in neutral, your car will start rolling uphill. The legend has it that the spirit of a woman who had crashed and died along that section of the road, is trying to push the car uphill to safety. Of course, there is a lot more logical and scientific explanation to this strange occurrence, and the supernatural has nothing to do with it. It is simply an optical illusion, nature playing tricks with our eyes. The vehicles at this particular point actually roll downhill; the slight decline looks uphill because of the surrounding landscape. The trees by the side of the road slant slightly down the hill and do not grow completely vertical; this confuses the senses and creates the illusion.

TRAINS, PLANES, & AUTOMOBILES

```
NAME:     The Chicken Gun
CODE:     TR8703
ORIGIN:   Unknown
STATUS:   False
```

The Chicken Gun

Every year, birds cause millions of pounds worth of damage to aircraft the world over. To combat the problem of birds damaging the windshield of aircraft, the US FAA (Federal Aviation Administration) have devised a device to test the strength of the windshields, and it is known as the 'Chicken Gun'. The Chicken Gun simply fires a chicken (already dead!) into the windshield of the aircraft at the same speed of which an aircraft would be travelling. If the windshield doesn't crack with the impact, it is safe to say that it would withstand a real collision in flight.

When British Rail was working on creating a new high-speed train, they asked the FAA if they could use the Chicken Gun to test the impact resistance of the windscreen on the proposed train. The first test went disastrously wrong as the chicken went straight through the windscreen, through the drivers seat, and made a huge indentation in the back wall. The BR engineers started from scratch and repeated the whole test, making sure that every instruction was carried out, but again the same thing happened. A third test was carried out, but again with the same results. Finally, the BR engineers gave up and resigned themselves to asking help from FAA. They told the FAA engineer the exact procedure of how they carried out the tests, and the disastrous results in detail. The reply was simple, "Next time, thaw the chicken first!"

Summary

The Chicken Gun does actually exist, and it is used to simulate flying birds to test the strength of different parts of an aircraft. The FAA first used a Chicken Gun in 1972 and the UDRI (University of Dayton Research Institute) from 1977. The UDRI reportedly fired frozen chickens at speeds up to 900mph, using a compressed gas gun with a 30ft long barrel. As time went on, the frozen chicken was substituted by a gelatine replacement that had the same mass and density as the chicken. Results are recorded and data is compiled using specialised cameras and lasers.

Now good people, this is the part where the truth gets a little hazy! The origins of this UL is unknown, but it dates back to at least 1986, and was covered by an Australian UL book in 1988. In the early versions, the frozen chicken was not fired by bungling English engineers, but by American jet engineers instead. As it stands, there has been no proof that the legend originated from an actual incident, and the origins of the legend are unknown. What is clear though, is that it has a condescending tone of superiority over less inferior foreigners to it. What I find interesting is that as the legend gets more Americanised as time goes on, the bungling engineers are no longer American, but have switched to being English, or any other European nationality. Now that is a surprise!

Final Thoughts

The threat of flying birds to aircraft is very serious, Heathrow London has a continuous problem of aircraft damage caused by Canadian Geese. The damage occurs during landing or taking off, when flocks of migrating Geese fly into the flight paths of aircraft.

On average, flying birds are considered responsible for the deaths of two aircrew members every three to five years, and reportedly cost the US Air Force between the sums of $50 to $80 million each year.

TRAINS, PLANES, & AUTOMOBILES

```
NAME:     The Road Hog
CODE:     TR8704
ORIGIN:   England, at least since 1970
STATUS:   False
```

The Road Hog

An old gent was taking his time driving along the narrow lanes that led into Bodmin (Cornwall), navigating the sharp turns with care and enjoying the scenery. Suddenly, a sports car comes hurtling around the corner; almost forcing the old man's Jag off the road and into a bush. As he swerved to avoid a collision, the young woman driving the sports car shouted, "PIG". The old man, who was now fuming, lent out of his window and shouted back at the woman "You stupid cow". Still smarting, the old gent carried on with his journey, and drove around the corner into a huge pig that was standing in the middle of the road!

Summary

The *'Road Hog'* is believed to have originated from England, and with the labyrinth style network of narrow and winding country lanes that scrawl across much of the countryside, the story is easy to relate to. Especially in Cornwall, where the roads look like the local drunk has designed them, with high hedges lining both sides of the winding roads, contributing to a high risk of a hazard around every corner.

This humorous UL is short and sharp, but as usual hides a sting in its tale. The old gent is very quick to take offence and retaliate verbally, to a comment that was no more than a warning to a hazard around the next corner, that the woman has just had to swerve to avoid. Perhaps the moral of this UL is that we shouldn't be too quick to judge, as some things may not be as they first appear.

Final Thoughts

Although first seen in print in England (1970), the legend spread across the Atlantic and became americanised in the 1980's. The American versions were usually based in Oklahoma, and the warning came from a farmer by the side of the road. Another variation similar to the English version has a woman shouting the warning, and the man replying, "You're not so great looking yourself!"

TRAINS, PLANES, & AUTOMOBILES

```
NAME:     Battle of the Ages
CODE:     TR8705
ORIGIN:   Unknown
STATUS:   False
```

Battle of the Ages

An old lady out doing her Christmas shopping had trouble parking her car, the place was packed and every car park space was taken. After circling around the car park at least a dozen times, she spots a man loading up his shopping into the back of his car. The lady drives over and parks near the space, waiting patiently for the man to finish loading his car. After what seemed like an eternity, the man climbed into the car and pulled out of the parking space. Before the lady even managed to put her Mercedes into first gear, a 'boy racer' in his Escort nipped into the space and started to walk away.

"Excuse me!" shouted the lady out of her window, "I've been waiting for that parking space!"

Without even looking back at her, the 'boy racer' responded, "Sorry lady, that's how it is when you're young and quick!"

Extremely annoyed, the lady slipped the Mercedes into first gear and rammed the Escort from behind, denting the rear bumper.

In total disbelief, the 'boy racer' shouted back, "You can't do that!"

The lady in the Mercedes said, "That's how it is when you're old and rich!"

Summary

With 'Road Rage' being the fashionable topic of the media, this story fits in with the current trend of low tolerance and violence on the roads. But 'Road Rage' is nothing new, and this UL was reportedly heard as far back as the 1960's and 70's.

The origins of this UL have not been traced, but the story has been told across Europe and the USA. When the legend is told it is often localised, and has normally happened to a friend of a friend (FOAF). The make of cars involved vary depending on the country and community of where the legend is based. In Britain, we stereotype the Escort as a 'boy racer' car, where in America the type of car is often a flashy Corvette. The lady always has an 'up-market' (executive) car, usually a Mercedes. The variations that involve the perpetrator's car being an old beat-up banger have an extra twist to the tale, as the lady chooses to smash her expensive car into the old banger just to prove a point, bringing credibility to the old saying 'cutting off your nose to spite your face'.

The very appeal of this UL is the fact that the arrogant punk gets his just deserts, and the old lady's fury is something we can all relate to. That smash up the bumper is for every dickhead that cuts you up in traffic, every jerk that jumps the queue in front of you when you have been waiting in line for ages, and for every German that creeps down in the middle of the night and puts their towels on the sun beds! After all, revenge is a dish best served cold!

Final Thoughts

A variation of this UL featured in a scene of the 1991 film 'Fried Green Tomatoes', which in turn was an adaptation of the novel by Fannie Flag.

A similar real life incident was captured by a CCTV camera in a multi-storey car park and shown on national television. A girl was waiting patiently for a car to pull out of a space, where the girl obviously wanted to park. But as soon as the other car had pulled out, a young bloke driving the wrong way through the car park nipped into the space, quickly got out of his car and walked off, ignoring protests from the girl. The footage then shows the girl returning to his car a while later, letting all the air out of his tyres until they are flat.

TRAINS, PLANES, & AUTOMOBILES

```
NAME:     Mr. Gay
CODE:     TR8706
ORIGIN:   Unknown
STATUS:   False
```

Mr. Gay

An airline engineer named Mr. Gay boarded an aircraft using his company pass. Finding that his designated seat was occupied and not wanting to cause a fuss, Mr. Gay sat down in an unoccupied seat nearby. Just before they were due to takeoff, another flight was cancelled, and the flight attendants were told that all non-paying passengers would have to disembark to make room for ticketed customers from the cancelled flight.

A flight attendant approached the man sitting in Mr. Gay's designated seat and asked, "Excuse me sir, are you Gay?"

The man, looking very surprised, answered, "Well, yes I am"

The flight attendant then responded, "I'm sorry sir, you will not be able to take this flight. Please collect your belongings and depart the aircraft."

The real Mr. Gay overheard the conversation and quickly interrupted, "I'm Gay". The flight attendant then instructed Mr. Gay that he would have to leave the aircraft.

Another man, observing the whole situation, suddenly stood up and defiantly announced, "I'm gay too. Heck, you can't throw us all off!"

Summary

I found myself hitting a brick wall on every turn trying to research the origins of '*Mr. Gay*', so I sought assistance from the respected '*Godfather*' of UL research, Prof. Jan H Brunvand. Replying to the E-Mail I sent him, he informed me that he cannot remember where he heard it first, but believes that it may have originated in Australia as well as the US. Prof. J H Brunvand went on to say that he believes that this story is more of a joke than a legend, and would be told as a joke, with some attempt at "Gay Speech Patterns" by many people.

I am also of the opinion that this is more of a joke than a legend, and the witty 'play on words' formula of this story would not look out of place on a TV comedy sketch show.

Final Thoughts

A similar version to this legend can be found in Prof. Jan H Brunvand's book titled 'Too Good Too Be True', page 122.

If any of you guys have any further information on the background of this UL, be sure to let me know!

TRAINS, PLANES, & AUTOMOBILES

```
NAME:     The Locked Out Pilot
CODE:     TR8707
ORIGIN:   1978, USA
STATUS:   False
```

The Locked Out Pilot

During the flight of a certain unnamed Airline, the pilot orders the co-pilot to take control of the aircraft while he speaks to some of the passengers in First Class. Everything was running smoothly, until the co-pilot desperately needed to use the toilet. He waited and waited for the Captain to return, until he got so desperate, he just had to relieve himself. Checking that the altitude was correct, and the sky was clear of traffic, he stuck the aircraft on autopilot and slipped out of the cockpit area and into the forward lavatory.

After relieving himself, the co-pilot went to open the door of the cockpit, only to find it locked. He fiddled around in his pockets trying to find the keys, before realising he had left them in his jacket pocket, hanging up in the cockpit area.

Not wanting to cause a fuss, the co-pilot calmly walked down the aisle and found the Captain, who was talking to one of the passengers. He asked the pilot if he could borrow his keys, to which the pilot replied that they were in his jacket. Immediately the Captain realises that they are both locked out of the cockpit and springs into action.

Both men ran back up the aisle and the Captain reached for the fire axe, and in front of horrified passengers, he chopped the door down. After the aircraft was brought back under control again, the embarrassed Captain explained to everybody what had happened over the speaker system.

Summary

Oral variations of this UL date back to at least 1978, and printed versions appeared in the mid 1980's. There have been many variations of *'The Locked Out Pilot'* over the years, but probably none quite so controversial as the version printed in the 'Chicago Tribune' travel section (Sunday, June 6th, 1999) where the story was told as an actual experience from the reporter Gabby Plattner. A Zimbabwe airline did not take kindly to its reference in the article as being the airline involved, as they thought it was damaging to their reputation and could affect the tourist trade of Zimbabwe. The author of the article quickly apologised and admitted that the story was not from her own experience, but one that she had heard of instead.

The number of flaws to this legend can only mean that this story cannot possibly be true. First of all, the cockpit area would never be left completely unattended at any time during a flight, and even it was, the cockpit's door would not be self locking, and so cannot be locked shut by accident. Even if the door did get locked accidentally, at least one spare key would be kept in a safe location somewhere else on board. The other obvious major flaw is that a fire axe would never be kept in a position where it could be used as a dangerous weapon, and is more likely to be kept in the cockpit itself.

Final Thoughts

The origins of *'The Locked Out Pilot'* are slightly murky and cannot be traced back to any particular incident. The first oral versions were usually told by members of the Airline trade to each other, and with this in mind, I believe that the legend originally started out as an 'in-house' joke amongst the airline industry.

TRAINS, PLANES, & AUTOMOBILES

```
NAME:      The Death Car
CODE:      TR8708
ORIGIN:    Prototype from Europe (From 1938 IN USA)
STATUS:    False
```

The Death Car   Version 1

A vintage Bentley had been sold for a meagre £1000! The reason for this is that the previous owner had been brutally murdered in a gangland killing while sitting in the front of the car, and the blood stains on the seat covers keep reappearing! The widow of the murdered man has tried everything from hand washing the covers to replacing them completely; the stains are seemingly removed at first, but reappear after a short period of time.

The widow was desperate to sell the car and brought the asking price down to a ridiculously cheap price after previous 'would be buyers' were put off by the reappearing stain. Even then she had problems selling the car, until a gentleman, who wishes to remain anonymous, bought the vintage Bentley for only a £1000.

The Death Car   Version 2

The owner of a red Corvette had driven out into the Nevada desert, parked up, and shot himself in the head. The body was left undiscovered in the car for a whole week, in temperatures well exceeding 100 degrees. After the police had discovered the body, the car was towed to the nearest garage.

As you can imagine, the heat of the desert had practically putrefied the dead body, and the stench from the car was immense. The whole of the interior was re-vamped and the Corvette was completely re-painted, but still the smell was unbearable. It was almost as if the stench had seeped into the metal framework, and no matter what they did, they couldn't get rid of the smell.

The going rate for a Corvette of this class is about $6000, but because of the stench, the dealer was forced to put the car on the market for only $500. To this day, the red Corvette has not been sold, the smell proving to be too unbearable for anybody to stand.

Summary

Version 1 is a typically English version of the '*Death Car*', and variations of the legend have been told up and down the country since at least the early 1950's. The English versions involve a stain and not a bad smell, this motif being more true to the prototype of the legend with bloodstains left at a murder site.

Version 2 is typically American, where variations have been traced back to 1938. In the American versions, the motif of why the car is hard to sell has evolved from a stain into a bad smell. The car cannot be sold no matter how low the price is brought down; the stench is just too much to bear.

The legend's prototype seems to have originated from Europe, and its roots stem back a lot further than 1938. As in *Version 1*, the problem was the bloodstains left by the murdered victim, but originally the crime site was not a car, this was only introduced as the legend evolved.

The make of the car varies depending on the location and period of time the story is being told in, but the chosen make and model is always a classic. Classic cars that have been used in this legend include a Cadillac, Jaguar, Bentley, Rolls Royce, MG, Ford Model A, Corvette and a Buick.

Final Thoughts

A rare 1959 'Eldorado Seville' Cadillac only has 2,232 miles on the clock, and was last driven on February 8th, 1959. On the night of that particular date, the flamboyant owner of the car, Maurice Gagnon, was kidnapped and shot to death in the car. The car has hardly been driven since, and still has the original battery, exhaust, and tires. After the Cadillac was pounded by the police as evidence, it was sold to a private collector, John Pfanstiehl, and is now kept at the Car Palace Museum in Massachusetts. Mr. Pfanstiehl was aware of the '*Death Car*' legend, and had serious doubts to the authenticity of the Cadillac before he saw it. Although this real life incident has many motifs of the '*Death Car*' legend, one vital one is missing; the car does not stink and does not have any bloodstains!

A classic episode of the comedy sitcom *Sienfield* featured this legend in '*Smelly Car*' in 1993, where a valets BO problem left an ineradicable smell in Jerry's car that made it undriveable and unsellable.

TRAINS, PLANES, & AUTOMOBILES

```
NAME:     The Bedbug Letter
CODE:     TR8709
ORIGIN:   1940's or earlier
STATUS:   Undecided
```

The Bedbug Letter

A lady on a business trip was making the long journey by train, and had retired for the night in a Pullman's sleeper. Half way through the night she had suddenly awoke feeling very itchy and uncomfortable, and with turning on the light she discovered that her bed was crawling with bedbugs. The lady immediately complained to the porter and asked to be given a new bunk to sleep in, only to be told that there were no vacant bunks left on the train.

After returning from her business trip, the lady wrote a furious letter to the railway company complaining of her ordeal. A prompt reply came back from the railway assuring the lady that hygiene has always been the top priority of the company, and that they were deeply apologetic for her experience. They went on to explain that the porter in her Pullman carriage had been disciplined, and that the whole carriage had now been fumigated. The letter finished by offering the lady a free railway ticket to a destination of her choice as compensation.

The letter was perfectly worded and was very apologetic and most sincere, it was even signed by the chairman of the railway himself. There was just one problem, attached to the top of the letter with a paper clip was an office memo note. Obviously meant for internal use only, it read 'send this whinging old cow the bedbug letter'.

Summary

The 'Bedbug Letter' was first reported from the 1940's, but may go back even further than that. It is unclear whether a true event triggered this legend, as the origins are completely unknown. A letter sent to the editor of *Princeton Alumni Weekly* February 5th, 1992 claimed the legend dates back to 1889 and claims it involves Mr. G Pullman (president of the Pullman Palace Car Company). There is no proof to back up the letter, and it is believed that the letter was written with the tongue firmly placed in cheek!

Modern variations of the '*Bedbug letter*' legend have moved to the skies, with the form of transport being aircraft. The complaint is normally about cockroaches, and the 'fob-off' letter has usually come from the Airline's Public Relations Manager, with a post-it note attached reading 'Send this jerk the Cockroach letter'.

This legend questions the sincerity of apology letters (known in the trade as *Duck* letters), and demonstrates the real thoughts of the company involved. In this case, a slick piece of PR (Public Relations) work is completely undone by a memo that was supposed to be for internal viewing only.

In old time Railroad slang, the term 'Bedbug' means a Pullman's Porter (a piece of totally useless information for you!)

Final Thoughts

In November 2000, Mr. Ian Payne, a nurse from Aylesbury, wrote to the BBC requesting a season of Jean Simmons films, and asked for the autograph of Lorraine Heggessy. The Beeb wrote back to Mr. Payne informing him that they could not consider a 'Simmons Season' at this time. Attached to the top of the letter was a post-it note reading, 'NUTTER, polite fob-off, no autograph.'

A spokesman for the BBC said: "We have apologised unreservedly to Mr Payne. We have tried to find out who wrote the 'post it' note and we have compared the handwriting from the officers and we cannot find anybody's handwriting that matches it. We are mystified at this."

TRAINS, PLANES, & AUTOMOBILES

NAME: Life Is Cheap
CODE: TR8710
ORIGIN: Unknown
STATUS: Undecided

Life Is Cheap

A friend of mine went to stay with relatives living in Nigeria. When reading the local newspaper he came across the heading 'Man flattened in road accident'. He thought that the wording was odd, and wondered why they didn't use a more traditional heading such as 'Man hit in road accident'.

After reading the news story, my friend understood the nature of the heading in sickening clarity; a car had knocked down a man and no one had stopped to help. Instead, the passing cars just treated him like road kill, driving over him until he was completely flattened into the ground!

After reading the article, my friend asked one of his relatives why people had not stopped to help or call an ambulance. Their reply was simply "Out here, life is cheap!"

Summary

My dad told me this story a few years ago and told me that one of his friends had told him the story, claiming it had actually happened to a friend of his. When we approached my dad's friend not so long ago, he couldn't recall telling the story and said it must have been someone else. Anyone who has ever attempted to trace the origins of a legend will have recognised this pattern. It is the old FOAF formula with the trail going cold before you have even started.

This is a great story that capitalises on the recent bad press that certain African areas can be dangerous places for tourists to visit. Although safari holidays are becoming ever more popular, some parts of Africa have been turned into no-go zones because of the high level of violent crime. This helps feed the notion that in certain African areas 'life is cheap'.

Final Thoughts

I do not know enough about this story to claim that I have uncovered a 'new kid on the block' UL, it may be safer to label it a proto-legend. Whether the legend grows only time will tell, but perhaps this publication will give it a helping hand!

TRAINS, PLANES, & AUTOMOBILES

```
NAME:     The JATO Rocket Car
CODE:     TR8711
ORIGIN:   Early 1960's; USA
STATUS:   False
```

The JATO Rocket Car

Police in Arizona were completely baffled after stumbling across the smouldering remains of a car embedded into the side of a cliff 150ft high! The damage to the car was so severe that the make and model could not be identified at the scene, nor how it got there!

After an intensive forensic and police investigation, the events that led up to the crash were gradually pieced together. A former member of the US Air Force was trying to beat the land speed record and had somehow got his hands on a JATO (Jet Assisted Take-Off) unit. JATO units are normally used on heavy military transport aircrafts to assist with their take-off, and are solid fuel rockets. Anyway, this bloke found a long straight stretch of road on the dried lake beds of Arizona, attached a JATO unit onto his 1967 Chevy Impala, then accelerated at high speed before switching on the JATO unit. The Chevy almost immediately reached a speed of up to 300 mph, and the driver would have experienced G-Forces normally associated with fighter pilots. After a couple of miles the driver would have been unconscious as the Chevy became airborne, the vehicle gradually climbing before impacting with the cliff face exactly 3.9 miles from where the JATO unit was first ignited.

The wreckage of the Chevy was so severe that the driver could only be identified by dental records, and his fingernails were found imbedded in what remained of the steering wheel.

Summary

This UL has reached cult status after becoming the Darwin Awards Winner of 1995, and has since become the most popular winner of the Darwin Awards of all time. A brief explanation to what the Darwin Awards is all about, is it's an annual honour given to the person who did the gene pool the biggest service by killing themselves in the most extraordinarily stupid way. Although this legend originally fooled the judges of the Darwin Awards, they have since recognised it as being a bogus story.

Although this legend has been given a new lease of life since being winner of the Darwin Awards, the origins go back a lot further than 1995. Original versions have reportedly been heard as far back as the early 1960's, where the car was a 1940's Ford, and the JATO was ignited to escape from pursuing cop cars along a Highway. The car ending up somewhere in the San Francisco Bay!

The legend was more widely spread in the 1970's, proving popular among the US Military Servicemen. These early versions explained how the JATO unit got into the wrong hands in the first place, usually explained as being taken from a cargo aircraft or air force base. This little background detail of how the JATO unit was obtained is noticeably missing in the latter day versions.

In the early 1990's, this gem of a legend had reached the vast arena of the World Wide Web, quickly establishing itself in cyberspace through the use of E-Mail. These versions were based in New Mexico, with a 'Plymouth Road Runner' being the make and model of the car involved. In 1995, the car was transformed into a 1967 Chevy Impala, and the location was switched to Arizona. The explosion of popularity that followed, firmly established this legend in Netlore history.

Final Thoughts

Is it just me, or does this UL remind you of that classic cartoon 'Roadrunner'? You know, the one where the coyote goes to extreme measures to try and catch the chirpy Roadrunner, but always ending up in spectacular failure. In some episodes, the Coyote would strap a large red rocket onto his back while wearing roller skates, when the Roadrunner zoomed past with his chirpy "Beep, Beep", the coyote would light the rocket hoping to catch up with the Roadrunner. This usually ended with the Coyote plummeting down to earth from the canyon, or colliding head first with a cliff face. Sound familiar, anyone?

TRAINS, PLANES, & AUTOMOBILES

```
NAME:     The Clever Motorist
CODE:     TR8712
ORIGIN:   USA; 1991
STATUS:   Undecided
```

The Clever Motorist

A man caught speeding on a Motorway by a speed camera, decided to play a little practical joke when he was sent his penalty fine of £40. He was also sent a photograph of the speeding car, the time and the date, and was informed that 3 points would be docked from his driving licence.

The motorist sent back a photo of a cheque payable to the amount of £40, the police then sent him a photo of a pair of handcuffs, the motorist got the message and paid up!

Summary

This British version of '*The Clever Motorist*' emerged onto the scene in 1997, but the story may have originated from a Newspaper column from a San Francisco columnist in 1991. Herb Caen told the story about Steve Barkley of Pebble Beach sending the police a photo of $45 dollars in cash, when fined the same amount after being caught speeding by a radar speed trap. A week later, the same columnist followed up the story, and reported that the police had outwitted Steve by sending him a photo of a pair of handcuffs. Caen finished the column by writing "Your move, Steve."

So, it seems that the legend could have emerged from a true incident, although I am not completely convinced of the authenticity of the Steve Barkley story, it seems to be too neatly constructed for my liking. Would the police have the time and patience to play this little game with Mr. Barkley? Or more than likely, would they not be amused by Steve Barkley's witticism, and consider it wasting police time?

The British versions to not vary a great deal from the American ones, although the photo sent to the police is normally of a cheque to the amount of the fine, not cash, as in the American versions. The legend is usually localised by the teller, and told as a recent event that has happened.

145

Final Thoughts

In Britain, motorists caught speeding by speed cameras have to request that photographic evidence is to be sent to them, at a cost of about £6 (at time of print). Photographic evidence is not sent automatically, as claimed in the British versions of the legend.

TRAINS, PLANES, & AUTOMOBILES

```
NAME:      The Wooden Airfield
CODE:      TR8714
ORIGIN:    World War Two
STATUS:    Undecided
```

The Wooden Airfield

During World War Two, the Germans built a decoy airfield in occupied Holland that was entirely made of wood. The 'airfield' was constructed with such detail that even the hangers, gun emplacements, oil tanks and aircraft were built entirely out of wood. The Germans spent so long building the decoy airfield that Allied photo experts had the time to observe and report it.

Finally, the last wooden plank was laid, and the decoy was at last finished. Any German celebrations were short lived though, as early the next morning, a lone RAF bomber crossed the Channel, came in low, circled the field once, and dropped a large wooden bomb.

Summary

This version of the popular wartime legend has been adapted from the book 'Masquerade: The Amazing Camouflage Deceptions of World War II', written by Seymour Reit, Signet, 1980. The legend was a popular tale amongst the allied forces, especially the RAF, and has been told ever since.

The truth behind the legend may be deeply entwined in wartime propaganda, and part of the psychological war that was being fought out between Churchill and Hitler. Stories like this were often used to boost the morale of the troops, and were deliberately spread amongst the forces during the war for this effect. If the legend were true, the mission carried out by the allied bomber would have been a risky propaganda stunt, carried out to demoralise the Germans and boost our own troops flagging morale. The stunt would have been carried out as a symbol of defiance, and a message to the Germans that the British cannot be outwitted.

The authenticity of the legend is in doubt because it is unlikely that the Germans would have spent so much time building a complex decoy airfield. The whole point of a decoy is deception, distracting the enemies away from the real target that may be miles away from the decoy. The bird's eye view from an aircraft would have been very limited, so only a simple two-dimensional structure would have been needed to achieve the deception. Another question is whether the allies would have risked an expensive aircraft and the life of a much-needed pilot just for a propaganda stunt? Risky missions were carried out for propaganda reasons, but it makes strategic sense to stay one step ahead of the enemy. The allies would have been far more likely to have played 'their cards close to their chest', not wanting to give anything away until the time was right.

Final Thoughts

Decoy airfields were used by both the British and the Germans, playing a vital role in the history of World War Two. To thwart the extensive damage caused by the Luftwaffe (German Air Force), the British built a complex array of decoy targets including airfields, placing them miles away from potential key targets. The aim was to fool the Germans into reporting back, and bombing, the decoy targets. With resources running low, the decoys also concealed the vulnerability of the deflated RAF at the time. The British drafted in a whole array of skilled workman to help construct the decoys, making them look as realistic as possible.

The decoy tactics proved to be successful as the decoy targets were bombed more than the real airfields, wasting thousands of tonnes of German bombs.

FOOD & DRINK...

INTRODUCTION...PAGE 150

KENTUCKY FRIED RAT..PAGE 151

AMERICAN SOUP...PAGE 154

BAR PEENUTS..PAGE 157

NEIMAN MARCUS COOKIES....................................PAGE 159

DON'T SWALLOW YOUR GUM...................................PAGE 162

COKECAINE...PAGE 164

SANTA COKE...PAGE 166

CARROT VISION..PAGE 168

PROJECT 2067

Wednesday 17th, August
11:00: At the Office

CATEGORY: FOOD & DRINK

What a stroke of luck! I had just about packed everything, except my toothbrush, ready for the journey home, when Max knocked on my apartment door early this morning. After what happened last night I was totally expecting a one-way ticket to London slapped across my face, but I was very surprised to what he had to say. It seems that Max is more than a little embarrassed with last nights' events, and would like me to erase the 'YMCA' episode totally from my mind. I think he feels that it will destroy his tough image and that he will never be able to live it down back at the office. The boys in the Print Room would certainly never let it lie. Of course I told Max that he needn't worry and that I would keep schtum, only I might need a few more days on the project to help me forget those disturbing images in my mind, and that will mean that my budget will have to be extended. Max agreed. Forgotten already!

I am glad and relieved that I have been given some extra days at such a crucial stage of the project. If Project 2067 had been shut down, all this hard work would have been for nothing. As it is we move onto the next Category called 'Food & Drink' which contains the *Kentucky Fried Rat* (FD3301), probably the most famous UL of all time. Another break-through legend for my project is *Carrot Vision* (FD3308), which gives a good insight into how Governments have realised the potential of UL's and have used them to maximum effect with wartime propaganda campaigns. On a personal note, I found *American Soup* (FD3302) both funny and interesting as my Kosovan friend explained to me how this legend was portrayed back in his homeland. It is a humorous look at the misunderstandings that can occur between two totally different societies. It has a similar tone to the story that when Polish immigrants first moved to America, they thought that dog food tins actually contained dog meat. This is because where they lived all tins had a picture on the front as a description of what they actually contained, so naturally they presumed that tins with pictures of dogs on them contained dog meat. It makes me wonder what they thought was in baby food!

FOOD & DRINK

```
NAME:     Kentucky Fried Rat
CODE:     FD3301
ORIGIN:   Early 1970's, USA
STATUS:   False
```

The Kentucky Fried Rat Version 1

A woman decided to treat her family to a take-away, and drove down to the local Kentucky Fried Chicken. On the way home, the smell of the chicken was too irresistible, and she pulled a piece of chicken out of the bucket to eat. She bit into the odd shaped piece of chicken, and immediately thought it tasted a bit strange. The woman pulled over to the side of the road, and switched the internal car light on to inspect the piece of chicken. After pulling away the crispy coating, she realised with full horror that the batter had been covering a dead rat. She had just bitten into a Kentucky Fried Rat!

The Kentucky Fried Rat Version 2

My friend's uncle bought a bucket of Kentucky Fried Chicken pieces before entering a cinema. When he had settled into his seat and the lights had dimmed, he decided to tuck into the bucket. He took a bite out of an odd shaped piece of chicken, and immediately felt some kind of strange ooze run out of his mouth and down his chin.

My friend's uncle spat out the mouthful of chicken and ran to the toilets to investigate, and was horrified when he saw blood running down his chin. He looked at the piece of chicken and saw what looked like a tale protruding from the crispy coating. On further investigation, he came to the sickening realisation that he had actually bitten into a batter-covered rat.

The Kentucky Fried Rat Version 3

Two young couples stopped one night for take-away chicken at a notable fast food outlet, and took their food back to the car. While sitting in the car eating their chicken, one of the girls complained that the chicken tasted funny. The driver switched on the light, and the girl discovered that she had been eating a dead battered rodent. The girl went into shock, and was immediately taken to the local hospital.

PROJECT 2067

Apparently, the husband of the sick girl was approached by lawyers representing the fast-food restaurant, and offered a tidy sum of $35,000. After several days, the girl was put on the critical list, the offer went up to $75,000, and this was refused. Unfortunately, the girl died, and the fast-food restaurant now has a huge lawsuit on their hands.

Summary

The *Kentucky Fried Rat* was first documented in the early 1970's, and since then it has become one of the most notorious and well loved UL's of all time. *Version 1* was heard in 1974, and is typical of the early US versions. Although the legend has proved to be versatile and there are many variations of the story, certain motifs remained the same. The fast food outlet was normally KFC, the battered creature was usually a rat, and the unlucky victim was usually a woman.

Version 2 was actually told to me by my good friend David Adams, sometime around the summer of 1990. I saw David a few months back and mentioned the story to him, and he still insists that it actually did happen to his uncle. In my friend's belief, I believe lies the key to the legend's success and popularity. The legend sounds so feasible, that, even the teller is convinced that the story actually happened. In other words, the legend is a typical 'Friend Of A Friend' (FOAF) tale. A phrase often used in the Urban Legend circles.

Details can differ from each variation, such as a mouse replacing the rat, and the name of the fast food chain or restaurant involved. Although, most variations target large corporate fast food franchises, and not locally run businesses. As in many UL's, the large corporate run businesses are seen as a faceless establishment, and a certain mistrust is shown towards the hygiene of fast 'assembly line' food.

Version 3 is an early example of the legend, taken from a documented version reportedly heard in 1971. This early version includes another important aspect to the legend; lawsuits. There have been many lawsuits over the years involving popular fast-food restaurants, but these have always involved parts of animals being found in food (such as when a battered chicken head was found in a box of Mc Donald's chicken wings by Katherine Ortega, in Virginia, USA). To my knowledge, not one case has involved a whole rat being found.

The Kentucky Fried Rat legend has a backhanded swipe at the speed and pace of modern society. We are more concerned with how quickly we can get, and eat our food, than the preparation of a nutritious and wholesome family meal. Fast food is used as a symbol of modern contemporary values.

Final Thoughts

The term 'Kentucky Fried Rat' is coined in the classic novel, 'The Beach' by Alex Garland. The main character uses the phrase to label the existence of a secret beach as an Urban Legend; he calls it a 'Kentucky Fried Rat Story'.

PROJECT 2067

```
NAME:     American Soup
CODE:     FD3302
ORIGIN:   Europe
STATUS:   False
```

American Soup

A man in Kosovo was regularly sent food packages from his relatives who had moved to America. One day, the postal service in his village telephoned the man to inform him that they had another package from America for him to collect. The man's car wouldn't start, so he had to ask his neighbour for a lift. The neighbour reluctantly gave him a lift into the village. The village was within walking distance, but he was afraid that the package would be too heavy to carry home.

When the man collected the package he almost died with embarrassment, as the parcel was no bigger than a can of beans. The neighbour cursed him for wasting his time and they went home.

Inside the package was a small tin of a greyish black powder substance. With delight, the man thought that his relatives had sent him some more of that delicious American soup that you only have to pour hot water onto. "Those clever Americans", the man said to himself, "They can turn soup into powder, and then the powder back into soup again". He wasted no time in making his soup, and although it didn't taste quite as nice as the other ones he had been sent before, he slurped it up with the same enthusiasm. Only after he had finished the last mouthful, the man spotted a small note that was attached with the package.

After reading the note, the man ran to the toilet and was violently sick. It appears that the note had informed him that his Aunt Mary had died, and that the package contained her ashes that they had sent back for burial in her homeland!

Summary

During a conversation about this legend, a good friend of mine told me this version. He is actually from Kosovo, and remembers hearing this story many times in his homeland, especially after the fall of the Communist state. He also informed me that the story was always told with a humorous tone, and was never taken seriously. Home grown stand-up comedians recited the story as part of their act, a tongue-in-cheek jibe at their own countrymen's blind bedazzlement of western technology and culture.

The Kosovan version circulated after the country was freed from the shackles of communism, and introduced to the western world. Throughout the '90's, people from this unstable, war torn country, have struggled bitterly against poverty. Many Kosovans have emigrated, or become refugees in other countries. Stories from these relatives about the western society have probably fuelled the legend.

This modern version of the UL, often referred to as 'Accidental Cannibalism', has parallel similarities to the original versions that became widespread in the years shortly after World War Two (WW2). In Britain, the war had taken its toll, money was scarce and food rations were in place for many years after. Powdered food was available under the ration restrictions, as well as being included in some relief packages. In other European countries, people had fled their homeland to escape persecution, and shipped back food to their poor relatives.

The true origins of the legend may have a more sinister anti-Semitic tone, from back in the days of the Renaissance. The story tells of an Italian Jew that smuggles his dead friends body back to Venice, by chopping the body into manageable pieces and pickling them in large jars with spices and honey. Then he transports the jars by boarding a ship bound for Venice. A Gentile from Florence, nicks a couple of pieces from the jars, and unwittingly feasts upon them!

'American Soup' is a story of misunderstanding between two very different cultures, and the difficulties that arise when a nation tries to adapt too quickly to an unfamiliar modern culture. It is also a story of unintentional cannibalism, of which, not only does the very thought conjures up powerful emotions of loathing and disgust, but also of thought provoking bewilderment.

Final Thoughts

In 1906, Upton Sinclair wrote a novel about the appalling conditions in Chicago's meatpacking industry. In one of the worst stories, a worker slips and falls into a large vat of meat being rendered for lard. The bones were eventually fished out of the vat, but the body had already been dissolved. This didn't stop

PROJECT 2067

production, and that batch of 'Durham's Pure Leaf Lard' was shipped out, bound for kitchen cupboards across America.

Stories like this one shocked the American public, and the U.S Department of Agriculture were forced to investigate whether the stories were true or not. They were true! Congress even had to call hearings to pacify an angry public, incensed that they had taken part in accidental cannibalism.

Radical changes were made to the law in the meat industry, culminating with America's first ever Meat Protection Act in 1906.

FOOD & DRINK

```
NAME:     Bar Peenuts
CODE:     FD3303
ORIGIN:   Unknown
STATUS:   Undecided
```

Bar Peenuts: **Version 1**

My sister and her boyfriend were visiting friends in Sri Lanka, and on one evening they all went to a local bar. Bowls of nuts were provided at the bar as free snacks, and my sister's boyfriend, never one to pass up an opportunity of free food, spent most of his time at the bar nibbling on nuts.

By the time the evening was out, my sister's boyfriend was complaining of stomach cramps, and was violently sick when they got back to their friends' house. He was also very ill the next day, and was baffled to what could have caused it. It was then that the friend's father told him a disturbing fact about bar nuts. Apparantly, a bowl of nuts had been taken away for analysis by health inspectors, and the results were shocking. On one single nut, they found traces of seven different kinds of urine! Of course, this is caused by people not washing their hands after they have been to the toilet.

My sister's boyfriend has vowed never to eat bar snacks again!

Bar Peenuts: **Version 2**

Health officials are urging restaurant owners not to hand out unwrapped mints to customers after a meal. The warning follows an investigation that found small traces of urine and fecal coliform bacteria in restaurant mint dishes.

Another study has revealed that 80% of people do not wash their hands after going to the toilet.

Summary

There is definitely some truth behind this UL, but how far the truth stretches is debatable. It is a fact that some States in America have ordered restaurants not to supply unwrapped courtesy sweets for their customers, unless it is done in an appropriate manner (e.g. using a dispenser machine). This action has been prompted by advice from health officials that unwrapped sweets could pose a health risk, and not based on any facts taken from an investigation.

Version 1 was actually told to me by my sister's boyfriend, and he really did become quite sick while they were on holiday. Although there is no proof that this was caused by eating the peanuts provided at the bar, he firmly believes that that was the reason. The very thought that the food could contain traces of urine sickens most people, but also seems very plausible. This may be because we know from our own experiences, that many people to not wash their hands after going to the toilet.

Version 2 is more like a news bulletin, and is more typical of the American versions. Generally, they are always backed up by research statistics, although the authenticity of the statistics is questionable. In the Straits Times Interactive, a reporter named Arti Mulchand wrote an article covering the subject. Arti claims to have done her own research by watching people go in and come out of a pub toilet. Arti claims that over half the people didn't wash their hands, and that included staff!

Final Thoughts

It is generally recognised that unwrapped sweets pose a health risk from not only unwashed hands, but also from other surrounding elements. Although our American friends have now opted for wrapped sweets, the British have not heeded the warning as many low star hotels and Indian restaurants have unwrapped courtesy mints in bowls.

Remember; always *wash* your hands!

FOOD & DRINK

NAME: **Neiman Marcus Cookies**
CODE: **FD3304**
ORIGIN: **At least since 1948**
STATUS: **False**

Neiman Marcus Cookies

My daughter and I had just finished a delicious salad at the Neiman – Marcus café in Dallas, and decided to have a small dessert. Being such cookie lovers as we are, we decided to try the 'Neiman – Marcus Cookie'.

The cookie was excellent, and I asked the waitress if I could have the recipe. With a small frown, she replied, "I'm afraid not."

"Well" I said, "Would you let me buy the recipe?"

With a cute smile, the waitress responded, "Yes." After asking how much, she responded, "Only two fifty, it's a great deal!" Amazed at how cheap the recipe was, I told the waitress to add it to my tab.

At the end of the month I received a visa statement from Neiman – Marcus, and was amazed that I had been billed $285.00. I had remembered that I had spent almost $10 on the two salads, and had bought a scarf for about $20. As I glanced at the bottom of the statement, it read 'Cookie Recipe - $250.00'. That's outrageous!

I immediately called Neiman's customer services department, and informed them that I had been quoted "two fifty" by the waitress, and under no interpretation does "two fifty" mean $250.00! Neiman – Marcus refused to budge. They would not refund my money, because according to them what the waitress had told me was not their problem. And because I had seen the recipe, there was no way that they could refund the money.

Angrily, I informed the woman on the other end of the phone that they could have my $250, but I was going to make sure that every cookie lover with an e-mail address would receive the recipe for free.

"I wish you wouldn't do that." The customer services woman replied.

PROJECT 2067

"Well, you should have thought about that before you decided to rip me off!" I responded.

So here it is!!

Please, please pass this recipe on to everyone you know. I paid $250 for this, and I don't want Neiman Marcus to get another penny for this recipe....

Summary

This classic piece of Netlore has been in circulation since at least 1989, and is usually found in the form of E-Mail. The example printed above is a typical E-Mail version, and is usually followed by the supposedly actual recipe for a Neiman Marcus Cookie. The legend has been totally debunked, and up to recently there was no such thing as a Neiman Marcus Cookie. In fact, Marcus Neiman only created a chocolate chip cookie through demand generated by the legend. Now that's what I call negative marketing!

Before setting its sights firmly on Marcus Neiman, the legend briefly targeted a Chicago department store named 'Marshall Fields'. Before that, in the 1980's, the legend was attached to the Mrs. Fields Company. Similar formula, except the misunderstanding about the "two fifty" took place during a request for the recipe over the telephone to the head office.

To find the true origins of the legend we have to look back a lot further than that though, possibly as far back as the 1930's to '40's. In fact, a similar story has been found in a cookbook dating back to 1948. The book 'Massachusetts Cooking Rules, Old and New' explains how a lady had asked a chef on a train for the recipe for the fudge cake that she was eating. The chef gladly sent her the recipe, and billed her $25. Her attorney advised her to pay the amount, so she sent the recipe to all her friends, hoping they would get some pleasure from it.

In the 1950's, the famous 'Red Velvet Cake' legend was born. This time, the spotlight was firmly fixed on the world famous Waldorf-Astoria Hotel in New York City. The legend tells of a woman who had had the Red Velvet Cake for dessert, and asked the management for the recipe. The hotel obliged, and sent her the recipe together with a bill of $300. Of course, she got her own back by sending out the recipe to everyone she knew. The legend hung over the hotel like a dark cloud, before moving on and attaching itself to the Mrs. Fields

FOOD & DRINK

Company in the 1980's. To combat the legend, the Waldorf-Astoria Hotel gives away the recipe for a Red Velvet Cake to anyone who asks for it – for free!

Final Thoughts

The following recipe for chocolate chip cookies can be found on the Neiman Marcus website. The website informs you that you can copy it, print it out, and pass it along to friends and family-and it's absolutely free!

NM Chocolate Chip Cookie Recipe

Ingredients

- 1/2 cup unsalted butter, softened
- 1 cup brown sugar
- 3 tablespoons granulated sugar
- 1 egg
- 2 teaspoons vanilla extract
- 1/2 teaspoon baking soda
- 1/2 teaspoon baking powder
- 1/2 teaspoon salt
- 1-3/4 cups flour
- 1-1/2 teaspoons instant espresso powder, slightly crushed
- 8 ounces semisweet chocolate chips

Directions

1. Cream the butter with the sugars until fluffy.
2. Beat in the egg and the vanilla extract.
3. Combine the dry ingredients and beat into the butter mixture. Stir in the chocolate chips.
4. Drop by large spoonfuls onto a greased cookie sheet. Bake at 375 degrees for 8 to 10 minutes, or 10 to 12 minutes for a crispier cookie. Makes 12 to 15 large cookies.

PROJECT 2067

```
NAME:      Don't Swallow Your Gum
CODE:      FD3305
ORIGIN:    Unknown
STATUS:    False
```

Don't Swallow Your Gum

HEALTH WARNING

Do not swallow Chewing Gum!

The gum is indigestible, which means your body cannot digest the gum. It will take a staggering seven years for the gum to pass completely through your digestive system.

Summary

The above message is a typical warning notice that usually takes form in the way of an E-Mail. Parents have been telling their kids not to swallow their gum for this very reason for years, and so the legend is nothing new. Chewing Gum is indigestible, and it is that term that has caused so much confusion. The simple fact is, that although swallowing your gum is not one of the healthiest of things to do, the gum will pass straight through your system, and into your stool undigested. Although experts argue that swallowing large amounts of sugar free gum could cause diarrhoea, this is because the sugar substitutes are not absorbed and pass into the small intestine and colon. So to sum it up, if you swallow gum, it will not stay in your stomach for seven years. But if you swallow an excessive amount of sugar free gum, it will give you the splats! Is that clear to every one?

I thought I would just touch on the history of chewing gum (for no apparent reason other than showing off my endless capacity for reeling off useless facts): Ancient Greeks chewed a form of mastic gum as far back as 50 AD. It was made from the resin obtained from the bark of the mastic tree, and was called Mastiche. The Greek women used the gum to freshen their breath and to clean their teeth.

The ancient Mayans of Central America also chewed the resin obtained from Sapota trees. The name of the resin was Chicle, and plays an important role in the history of chewing gum.

FOOD & DRINK

During the 1860's, an unusual partnership formed the origins of the modern chewing gum. Antonio Lopez de Santa Anna, several times president of Mexico and famed for orchestrating the bloody battle of Alamo, introduced Chicle to Thomas Adams, a New Yorker. The idea was to use Chicle as a rubber substitute, but history had other plans, as it was found to be more useful as a base for chewing gum. This proved to be the benchmark for the modern chewing gum.

Final Thoughts

New research shows that chewing gum could increase your brainpower! In a joint study carried out by the University of Northumbria and the Cognitive Research centre in Reading, results showed that chewing gum increased thinking power and improved memory.

In experiments, people who had been chewing gum had an increased heartbeat of three beats a minute faster than those who hadn't chewed gum. This is probably because the chewing action improves the delivery of glucose and oxygen to the brain, which would make the person more alert.

Another theory is that chewing gum causes a surge of insulin, due to the mouth watering in anticipation for a meal. There are Insulin receptors in the brain, which are important for learning and memory.

PROJECT 2067

```
NAME:     Cokecaine
CODE:     FD3306
ORIGIN:   1885
STATUS:   True
```

Cokecaine

Cocaine was used in the recipe of the original Coca-Cola drink.

Summary

It's hard to believe, but the class 'A' drug, Cocaine, was used as part of the original Coca-Cola formula. Coca-Cola was given it's name in 1885, and was marketed as a tonic for most common ailments, based on the two medicinal main ingredients which consisted of extracts of Coca leaves and Kola nuts. The exact amount of Cocaine that was used in the original recipe is not certain, but only after a few years, the amount was dropped considerably. The reason being that by the mid 1890's, the harmful effects of Cocaine were now being realised and the use of Cocaine was starting to be frowned upon. It is reported that Coca-Cola still had to include traces of the drug as an ingredient, to protect the trade name of the drink. The 'Coca' part of Coca-Cola was a descriptive reference to the Cocaine (Coca Leaves) that the drink's syrup contained. So, to protect the rights to the name of Coca-Cola, the drink had to contain cocaine. In the early days, the syrup had not been patented, so the name was a very valuable asset.

The exact year that Coca-Cola stopped using Cocaine as an ingredient completely is not certain, as the year varies considerably from source to source. It is widely believed that all traces of the drug were removed from the formula in 1905, but another source also reports that Cocaine was not completely removed until the late 1920's.

Final Thoughts

This legend is part of a much bigger group of Urban Legends, commonly known as 'Cokelore'. The global success of the Coca-Cola Company has been tremendous and spectacular to say the least, and the amount of UL's associated with Coca-Cola is a fair reflection to that success. Probably, the only other

FOOD & DRINK

company that could claim such a sheer volume of legends associated with it is Disney.

Cokelore legends range from the truth, to the ridiculous, and include such classics as Coca-Cola used to be green, claims that the Mormons own the company, and a mouse was found in a Coke bottle. In case you were wondering, the first two are most definitely false, but the mouse in the bottle may be based on an actual true event (scary thought!)

PROJECT 2067

```
NAME:     Santa Coke
CODE:     FD3307
ORIGIN:   1930's
STATUS:   False
```

Santa Coke

Coca-Cola originally created the modern day image of Santa Claus as an old, tubby, but jolly man, dressed in a red and white robe. The image was part of a seasoned Coca-Cola advertising campaign, and has Santa Claus wearing their corporate colours of red and white.

Summary

The familiar image of Father Christmas (Santa Claus) is known throughout the world, and is probably the most familiar symbol of Christmas. But things haven't always been that way, and the history of the big chubby fella is a complex mixture taken from different myths, legends, and stories.

The modern day Santa Claus has been moulded from two separate religious traditional figures. The first is St. Nicholas, the Elf like gift bringer, and the second is Kriss Kringle. Kriss Kringle derives from the name 'Christkindlein', which means 'child of Christ', and was part of tradition over much of mainland Europe. The American version of Santa Claus originates from the Dutch tradition of 'Sinter Klaas', which was introduced to America by Dutch settlers in New Amsterdam (now known as New York). The tradition of Sinter Klass is based on the myth of St. Nicholas, and the Dutch tradition picked up momentum when the New York Historical Society was founded in 1804, with St Nicholas as it's patron saint.

In 1823, Clement C Moore wrote a poem for his children titled 'A Visit From St. Nicholas'. The poem was later published, and included the now legendary picture of Santa Claus by Thomas Nast. The poem and the picture are probably one of the most prominent factors in forming the modern day Santa Claus.

The American image of Santa Claus only became standardised after the British tradition of Christmas Cards was introduced to America, which in 1885 donned the familiar red and white suited Father Christmas.

The Coca-Cola Company first used an image of Santa Clause in their advertising during the 1920's, and was used with adverts in magazines. The image of the Santa they used was similar to the work of the caricaturist, Thomas Nast, and was rather stern and serious looking.

In 1930, Santa appeared in the seasoned Coca-Cola advertising campaign again, this time the artist Fred Mizen painted a department store Santa that was used in print ads. The campaign was successful, but Coca-Cola wanted a more realistic and symbolic Santa Claus for the next campaign.

In 1931, Coca-Cola turned to the talented Haddon Sundblom for their seasoned advertising campaign. Sundblom wanted a warmer, friendlier, and more approachable Santa, and so turned to Clement C Moore's poem 'A Visit From St. Nicholas' for inspiration. The results were a slightly plump, jolly, and elf like Santa. Haddon Sundblom painted these Santa Claus portraits for the next 35 years.

As far as I am aware, Coca-Cola do not claim that they created the modern image of Santa Claus, merely that they helped create it; which is arguably true. The modern image of Santa may have been moulded from Clement C Moore and Thomas Nast, but it was Haddon Sundblom's vision and Coca-Cola's mass commercialism that standardised the image of Santa Claus globally.

Final Thoughts

Of course, in Britain we have our own Father Christmas, who differs slightly in appearance from Santa Claus, as he has a longer beard and coat. The legend of Father Christmas originates from Finland, where it's roots is in an old Pagan tradition. The original Joulupukki (Father Christmas) was a frightening creature that didn't give presents, but demanded them instead. Over the years, with the influence of Christian beliefs and local traditions, the Joulupukki was moulded and transformed into the lovable Father Christmas we know and love today.

PROJECT 2067

```
NAME:     Carrot Vision
CODE:     FD3308
ORIGIN:   World War Two
STATUS:   True
```

Carrot Vision

By utilising the old folktale that eating carrots will help you to see in the dark, the British RAF managed to fool the Germans and disguise the use of Radar during World War Two. The story goes that the RAF bragged that the great accuracy of their fighter pilots at night was the result of them being fed enormous quantities of carrots. In actual fact, the successes of the RAF pilots were entirely due to the highly efficient newly installed onboard radars! The Germans bought the story because their folk wisdom incorporates the same myth about carrots as ours.

Summary

So it seems that the line, "Eat up your carrots, it will help you see in the dark", was not only used by our own mum's to nag us when we were younger, but the Germans have obviously had the same problem. There were other logical reasons why the Germans bought the story so easily, but I will come to that in a minute. First, I would like to explain the importance of radar, and the impact it had during the war.

World War Two was unique in many ways, one of them being that it was the first war where intelligence and information was recognised as a powerful tool in the art of strategy and tactics. At times, it was almost as if Hitler and Churchill were playing the war like a game of chess, each one trying to guess the other ones move and counter attack. With this in mind, perhaps you can understand the importance of the invention of Radar. Before Radar, advanced warning of enemy aircraft depended solely on how quickly they were visually spotted. Radar cut the response time, and made it easier for allied pilots to locate and intercept enemy aircraft. When Radar systems were fitted onto allied Bombers, night raids into enemy territory could be made with a high level of accuracy. With such advancement in the war of technology, you can understand that it was in British interests to keep one step ahead of the game.

FOOD & DRINK

It is not completely clear whether the rumours spread about the pilots eating huge amounts of carrots was used to disguise the success of the interception of enemy nightly raids, or for the highly accurate allied night time bombing raids on enemy territory. I believe it was the latter, and I will explain why. In 1942, the GEE system was introduced. The GEE system was a pulse phasing Radar system, with the receiving equipment fitted on board aircraft. It was the first Radar device to be installed on Bombers, and was used as a navigational aide during nightly raids. The use of the GEE system was a success, and the government were intent on keeping the use of the system top secret and out of enemy hands.

So, to keep the Germans guessing, the British government used a smoke screen with the use of the rumour. Just like in *Wooden Airfield* (TR8714), the British government realised the potential and power of UL's when used as part of wartime propaganda. But, as I have already said, the old myth about carrots was not the only reason why the Germans fell hook, line and sinker for the rumour. The German intelligence also knew that the British had been experimenting with high carotene roots varieties to try and reduce the effects of night blindness for pilots. Because of the experiments, the British had a large stock of carrots, and cleverly used this fact to fuel the rumour that the RAF pilots had developed superb night vision due to the consumption of large amounts of carrots!

Final Thoughts

So, I bet you are wondering whether the old myth about eating carrots is true (well, tough, I am going to tell you anyway!) To answer that question bluntly, no. But, having said that, carrots contain a reasonable amount of Vitamin A. Vitamin A is vital for our body, and lack of it could lead to blindness and defective growth.

AROUND THE WORLD...

INTRODUCTION..PAGE 172

THE GUCCI KANGEROO.....................................PAGE 174

FLATJACK...PAGE 176

HONEYMOON HORROR.....................................PAGE 178

FLYING COWS..PAGE 180

SOUNDS LIKE ENEMY WHALES.....................PAGE 182

VOTE DONALD DUCK!.....................................PAGE 184

THE ITALIAN JOB..PAGE 186

THE BELGIUM BEAST......................................PAGE 188

CLEANING UP WITH TOOTHPASTE...............PAGE 190

HOME IS WHERE THE AIRPORT IS.................PAGE 192

TWO FINGER SALUTE......................................PAGE 195

PROJECT 2067

Wednesday 17th, August
16:00: Just finished being interviewed by cops

CATEGORY: AROUND THE WORLD

My office has been broken into! I made the discovery after popping out for a greasy samosa for lunch. When I came back everything seemed as normal, there was no sign of forced entry, nothing appeared to have been taken and the place wasn't trashed. In fact, I only noticed that there was something wrong when I realised that my papers and files were a lot tidier than usual. I have heard about these weirdo's in Germany who break into peoples houses while they are at work and perform a complete spring clean without taking anything, and my immediate response was that I have had the same treatment (I wondered that if I had left the keys to my apartment, they would do the same there as well!). I then realised that somebody was looking for something and had tried to cover their tracks. Big mistake, if they had trashed the place I might not have even noticed anyone had been there!

The riddle of how somebody managed to get into my office without breaking the door down or tampering with the lock became clear after I had informed the building's security. Apparently, a man posing as my brother had tricked a cleaner into opening my office door, claiming that he wanted to surprise me when I came back from lunch. This building has CCTV, security guards, reinforced doors with a double bolt lock for every office (including my shoebox), yet, somebody posing as my brother can just walk in off the streets and straight into my office by outwitting the half-brained cleaner. They might as well have rolled out the red carpet for the intruder and invited him in for tea and shortcakes!

I can't be sure what the intruder was looking for, but if it was anything to do with Project 2067, he was out of luck as I had all the Project's documents with me in my briefcase. What disturbs me is *who* would want my documents and for what purpose? Perhaps my investigations into cover-ups, government propaganda and conspiracies have ruffled a few feathers. How serious are these people and what kind of danger am I in? If I do not report in tomorrow I have probably been killed by a crazed lone gunman who has managed to shoot at me from various positions at the same time, including a grassy knoll. Anyway, the show must go on, so lets have a look at the next category.

This category is a round trip cruise that will let you explore UL's from across the four corners of the earth. We have the *Gucci Kangaroo* (AW1801) from down

AROUND THE WORLD

under. An amusing tale with many variations, and has now been made into a feature film. We have an absolutely horrific offering from Japan called *Honeymoon Horror* (AW1903), which explores the very real and gruesome trade of human trafficking. Nearer home in Europe we have the *Belgium Beast* (AW1908), an amazing and ridiculous tale that mixes the anti-Christ with big brother (you have to read it to believe it!). Nearer home still, we have the remarkable but true story of a refugee who has been stranded at the Charles De Gaulle Airport in Paris for more than a decade in *Home Is Where The Airport Is* (AW1910).

This selection of UL's in Around The World is but a mere sprinkling compared to the mass volume in circulation worldwide. I suppose you could say that this is more of a fly-over than a cruise, a tiny glimpse of what this category has to offer. It would be impossible to cover all the legends from around the world, as each country has such a vast and rich supply of national legends that have been embroidered into the very fabric of their own societies. To give this category justice, a book of legends from each and every country would need to be produced. Perhaps something to do on a rainy afternoon!

UL's can be a useful tool in understanding the different cultures of a country as they often represent the views, politics, fears and anxieties of the people. In other words, to understand what makes different cultures tick; one of the best sources of information is UL's.

PROJECT 2067

```
NAME:     The Gucci Kangaroo
CODE:     AW1901
ORIGIN:   1902, Australia
STATUS:   False
```

The Gucci Kangaroo: Australia

During the Americas Cup, held in the waters of Perth, Western Australia, a group of Gucci representatives who were sponsoring the Italia yacht team decided to look for Kangaroos to kill time in between races. They had cruised the outback all afternoon trying to spot a *'Roo'*, and had just about given up when a Kangaroo jumped out straight in front of their Land Rover. Unable to avoid the unfortunate animal, they skidded into the *'Roo'*, knocking him down with a bone shuddering thud.

Instead of feeling saddened by the dreadful accident, the Italians felt quite pleased with their catch. They propped the motionless Kangaroo up against the side of the Land Rover, dressed him with a pair of sunglasses and one of the representative's Gucci jacket, and began taking photos.

It was at this point that the startled animal (only stunned) jumped up and bounded off, still wearing the sunglasses and jacket. The loss of an expensive jacket wouldn't have been so bad, if the Land Rover's keys had not been placed in the inside pocket!

Summary

The earliest found version of this UL dates back to 1902 from Australia, and was traced to a book called 'Aboriginalities' by Australian folklorist Bill Scott. In that version a train and not a car knocked out the 'roo', and of course he didn't make off with a Gucci jacket to add to his collection. In fact, the Kangaroos must have quite an extensive collection judging by all the variations to the legend. Over the years they have not only bounded off with Gucci jackets, but also Ray Ban sunglasses, expensive cameras, baseball caps, crew jackets, passports and expensive jewellery to add to their collection. I think the Kangaroos are setting themselves up for quite a jumble sale out there in the outback!

The Italians are not the only callous foreigners who got their just desserts. 1950's versions were told about the English cricket team, and in more recent years, the

Canadian yacht team. All these versions underline mistrust towards foreigners, highlighting the lack of respect and callousness shown towards the host nation. Just for a cheap prank, the foreigners act disgracefully and pay the price. The Kangaroo gets the last laugh, and that's fair dinkum' mate!

During the 1960's the UL hit celebrity status, and became associated across America with the "The Kingston Trio". The Kingston Trio were a popular folk-singing group, and one member told the legend as a personal experience that had actually happened to them while the group were touring Australia.

Final Thoughts

Another similar American UL exists that is very similar to this one, and it is called the *'Deer Departed'*. The story goes that while a man is hunting in a forest, he manages to shoot down a deer with huge antlers. He set up his camera on a tripod and posed with the animal, placing his expensive high-powered rifle with its telescopic sight across the deer's antlers. Only stunned, the Deer jumps back onto it's feet and bounds off into the forest, with the rifle still firmly placed between its antlers!

The 'Animals revenge' stories may have originated from the late 1890's, when the stories were rife in both America and Australia. These tales were normally about a cruel man who ties a stick of dynamite to the tail of an animal (e.g. dog, coyote, rabbit) as an evil prank. The joke always backfires when the animal runs back into the man's house!

PROJECT 2067

```
NAME:     Flatjack
CODE:     AW1902
ORIGIN:   S. Africa
STATUS:   False
```

Flatjack – S. Africa

A young lady was driving her 4x4 jeep along a long stretch of road on the outskirts of Johannesburg that is notorious for carjackings, when she suddenly saw an abandoned car, sideways on, in the middle of the road right in front of her. Realising that this may be a ploy by carjackers to stop her car, she stepped on the accelerator and swerved off the road onto the bumpy grass shoulder, skidding back onto the road after she had passed the abandoned car. When reaching home, the woman phoned the police and told them what she had seen. Thinking that was the end of it, she went to bed.

Early the next morning, the lady was awoken by the police wanting more information on what had actually happened the previous evening. She told them in great detail of how she had taken her 4x4 off the road at speed, passing the abandoned car by driving on the long grass verge, and skidding back onto the road. The police then informed the lady that in doing so, she must have run over and killed three men who were lying in wait to ambush her.

Summary

Carjacking is a relatively new phenomenon in Britain, with a very small percentage of cases ending in murder. S. Africa is different, and has the highest carjacking rate in the world. In a country that has a population of 40 million, there are roughly 16,000 carjackings a year, and 57 of those will end in a person being murdered. In comparison, the ratio of carjackings is 18 times greater than the USA. So you can see why carjacking in S. Africa is taken as a very serious threat, and as always, UL's are used to express this fear.

This legend was rampant throughout the mid 1990's, widely known throughout the whole of S. Africa. In a country that is gripped by so much fear of the crime, it is not hard to see why a legend that gives a sense of poetic justice is so popular. The accidental death of the would-be carjackers rings some truth in the saying 'what goes around comes around'.

Final Thoughts

The fight against carjacking has been cranked up a notch or two by fed up South Africans, and there are plenty of courses to attend that teach you the best ways in dealing with a situation if it happened to you. Advice includes always keeping the car doors locked when travelling, and for woman to keep their car rolling even at traffic lights showing red. Statistics show that the most vulnerable time for motorists are between the times of 16.00 and 20.00, just before it gets dark. Tuesdays and Fridays are the day's motorists are most likely to encounter a carjacking. The most vulnerable places have proved to be driveways, supermarkets, schools and traffic lights.

Where conventional methods have failed in the fight against carjacking, South Africans are turning to ever more ingenious weapons and gizmos for protection. Such items include a flamethrower that shoots out of the driver's side door, a shotgun device that is mounted under the driver's seat and can be operated by remote control, and a chassis mounted spring-loaded sword!

PROJECT 2067

NAME: Honeymoon Horror
CODE: AW1903
ORIGIN: Japan
STATUS: False

Honeymoon Horror: Japan

A newly wed couple from Japan went to Thailand for their honeymoon and decided to go shopping for clothes. The young wife spent many hours looking for dresses, and found a few that she liked in a trendy looking fashion store. She went to the dressing room to try them on, while her husband waited outside.

After a long while, the husband became anxious that his wife hadn't reappeared from the dressing room, and asked a member of staff to investigate. What they found was that the girl had simply disappeared! After a lengthy police investigation, to no avail, the young Japanese man had given up hope of ever seeing his wife again, and went back to Japan a broken man.

Five years passed. The man had just about got over the disappearance of his wife and had managed to piece his life back together, when a friend who had been on holiday in the Philippines claimed to have seen the man's wife. With regret, the friend told the man that he had seen his wife in a sex freak show, with both her legs and her arms horribly mutilated.

As it happens, the dressing room where the wife had disappeared had a trapdoor to the floor below. A well-organised gang of kidnappers were waiting below, and she had been sold into a prostitution ring.

Summary

This incredible tale is widespread across Japan, and certainly seems to feed on fears of abduction. Although tales of abduction are common throughout the world, in Japan they are told with a little more conviction, to the extent that girls warn each other about trapdoors in changing rooms when shopping alone.

The fact that most Japanese variants of this legend happen in a foreign country, probably suggests a deep-rooted mistrust of the outside world and an uncertainty of foreign cultures. Although, it must be said that the legend is very similar to

AROUND THE WORLD

other American and European UL's, where girls are kidnapped in clothes shop changing rooms and sold into 'white slavery' for use as prostitutes.

Final Thoughts

The reality of this UL actually happening is very unlikely, but the fears behind the legend are completely justified. Human trafficking has become a problem the world over, and the gangs behind it are extremely well organised. These gangs prey on the vulnerable, often targeting girls from poor backgrounds. They are lured abroad by promises of money and jobs, and then sold into prostitution rings. Once abroad, they are trapped. The girls cannot escape, as they have no money, papers, or passports, and live under constant fear from their capturers.

PROJECT 2067

```
NAME:      Flying Cows!
CODE:      AW1904
ORIGIN:    Unknown
STATUS:    False
```

Flying Cows! – Russia

A Russian rescue crew plucked some Japanese fisherman from the sea after their vessel had capsized. The Russian authorities quickly detained the fishermen when they claimed that flying cows had sunk their vessel!

The story sounded ridiculous, until Russian investigations began unravelling a bizarre set of events that led to the vessel being sunk by cows falling from the sky.

Apparently, a couple of Russian Air Force members decided to smuggle a couple of cows back home from a Serbian airfield, by hiding the animals in the bomb bay of their aircraft. Everything was fine until the aircraft reached and cruised at a colder altitude, and then the cows went berserk.

To save themselves and the aircraft, the crew hastily decided to open the bomb hatch, dropping the cows thousands of feet onto the deck of the unfortunate vessel down below.

Summary

Flying cows-I love it! The legend has been around for years, but only reached notoriety when the German Embassy in Moscow reported the story to the German Foreign Ministry in Bonn in the mid nineties. A German newspaper got hold of the story and printed it.

The legend bursting onto the scene at this particular time may be the influence of a popular Russian film of the time called *Osobennosti Natsionalnoi Okhoty* (catchy name!), which features a similar story.

The film cannot be credited for the legend though, as this UL had been recorded and printed may times before the film was even made. The *Moscow Times* printed an article on the story on 1st June 1990. The Russians have also told the story as a joke for years.

Final Thoughts

The legend may have originated from a similar story heard in Scotland, 1965. A driver explains rather gingerly to police how a flying cow landed on the bonnet of his car, causing him to crash. Relieved police told him that a lorry driver reported hitting a cow, but couldn't find the body anywhere. The speed and weight of the lorry must have sent the cow flying a considerable distance back down the road, landing on the bonnet of the gentleman's Austin.

PROJECT 2067

```
NAME:      Sounds Like Enemy Whales
CODE:      AW1905
ORIGIN:    Unknown
STATUS:    Undecided
```

Sounds Like Enemy Whales – Sweden

Swedish naval experts were convinced that foreign submarines were operating in Swedish waters, and the foreign secretary made a strong worded speech at a UN Conference. Despite this, no foreign government claimed responsibility for using submarines in Swedish waters. The Swedish government decided to launch a massive naval operation to uncover the perpetrators.

After weeks of searching the waters and a painstaking task of tracking sonic sounds under the sea, it was concluded that the perpetrators were not enemy submarines, but a school of whales. Even so, the Vice-Admiral of the Swedish Navy is still convinced that foreign submarines are operating in Swedish waters.

Summary

This wonderful legend may, or may not be true, but it certainly touches on a sensitive subject of underwater noise pollution. It has been reported that certain types of marine life, including mammals such as whales, are directly affected by the low frequency sounds omitted from machinery in ships and submarines, and the low frequency sonar sounds sent out to detect enemy submarines. Sonar sounds have been used by ships since World War Two, but advances in technology and the development of near silent submarines has meant that a new active sonar has been developed to bounce off submarines instead of waiting until the submarines are close enough to hear. The problem with this is that the low frequency sonar sounds cause havoc amongst the marine life. Whales depend on sound as we depend on sight, and they use sonar sound to find food, attract a mate, detect enemies, and to communicate with their young. The man-made sonar sounds can interrupt and drown out these natural sounds, and can even cause deafness, disrupt migration patterns, and at worse cause death amongst the whales.

Another aspect of this legend is the UL concept of being *baffled by technology*. Despite the ever-increasing advances in technology, we are still all prone to human mistakes. The concept that the sonar sounds given from submarines and that of whales must be very similar, is given creditability from another fact; that, after the cold war had ended, the US Navy handed over its supersensitive hydrophones to a research project called *Whales '93*. This equipment now used for monitoring whales, was first used as ears looking out for enemy submarines.

The debate concerning the use of high intensity active sonar systems has been turned up a few notches during the last few years, with the news that the US Navy intend to use a new high intensity active sonar system to detect and track enemy submarines. According to Navy sound charts, the LFAS signal can be 140db when more than 300 miles from its source. It is claimed that this has caused the death of whales from brain haemorrhage and it could affect all species of marine mammals. It is also claimed that NATO are also developing a similar system, along with many other countries. This brings fresh concerns over the impact of marine life when all these systems are used simultaneously on a cumulative level.

Final Thoughts

In another bizarre news story that has *supposedly* been reported by the Times, the Soviets have sold 27 naval amphibians to Iran. The amphibians, which include dolphins and beluga whales, have been trained by the Soviet military, and have been sold as part of a mass post cold war sell-off.

The amphibians have been trained to distinguish between the sounds of friendly or enemy submarine engines, and can even locate missing torpedoes and missiles.

I must admit, this news story smells *fishy* to me.

PROJECT 2067

```
NAME:      Vote Donald Duck!
CODE:      AW1906
ORIGIN:    Sweden
STATUS:    False
```

Vote Donald Duck!

The results of the Swedish General Election a few years ago caused much controversy. The Social Democrats, Conservative, and Green Party fared as expected, but some of the other voting results caused uproar amongst politicians in the Riksdag (Swedish Parliament).

For some peculiar reason, nearly 13,000 people cast their vote to Donald Duck, which is nearly enough votes to win a seat in the Riksdag. Other strange results included Keith Richards (Rolling Stones) with 14,000 votes, Mick Jagger (also Rolling Stones) with 500, Bill Gates with 250, and the Pope with 100 votes. Flagging well behind was the "Queen of Pop" herself, Madonna, with 1 vote!

Summary

I decided to stay with Sweden a while longer, as this UL really is too good to pass by. Although claimed by many to be true (including reputable websites), the simple truth is that Donald Duck did not receive 13,000 votes. Sofia Knap of the Election Authority in Sweden also informed me that even if he had, it would not have been enough to gain a seat in the Riksdag. Although these details are not correct, there is a political party in Sweden called the "Donald-Duck-Party".

This UL is widely believed because the Swedish voters used to have the right to freely erase or add names of their choice on the voting slip. The voting system has since been revised, and the voters no longer have these rights.

I would like to know why Keith Richards is claimed to have got a staggering 13,500 more votes than fellow band member Mick Jagger, and Madonna must be disappointed with her result!

Final Thoughts

Why Donald Duck? In one source of information, I read that over the Christmas period, the Swedes traditionally watch Donald Duck cartoons on TV. It is as traditional for them as the Queen's speech and eating mince pies is to us.

Perhaps somebody should inform the Swedes that Donald Duck is just a character from a CARTOON, and he is NOT REAL. Mind you, I can see the attraction of Donald Duck over most politicians!

PROJECT 2067

```
NAME:      The Italian Job
CODE:      AW1907
ORIGIN:    Italy
STATUS:    Undecided
```

The Italian Job

An Italian family living in a village near the border with Slovenia decided to cross the border one evening for a fish meal at a cheap local tavern they knew of. After travelling a few miles into Slovenia, the family were stopped by a group of soldiers and ordered out of the car. The heavily armed men took their coats and seized the car, driving off leaving the family stranded on a remote road.

After half an hour the soldiers returned, apologised for the mistake, and gave back the family's possessions including the car. The soldiers warned the family that they should return to Italy immediately.

A few miles down the road, the family noticed a funny smell coming from the back of the car. They pulled over to investigate and were horrified when they discovered two dead bodies inside the boot!

Very frightened, and in a state of panic, the family discarded the bodies by the side of the road, and sped off home as quickly as possible.

Summary

In the spring of 1993, this horrific tale spread rapidly amongst Italian towns and villages close to the northern border with Slovenia. It was a time of great political unrest in the ex-Yugoslavian regions, and I think that this UL demonstrates the mistrust and vulnerability felt amongst Italians living close to the border of their fellow neighbour. The fact that this UL surfaced at a time when Slovenia were no longer at war throws questions about the professionalism and conduct shown by Slovenian soldiers, portraying them as corrupt and ill-disciplined.

This tale has parallel similarities with such legends as *"The Body In The Bed"* (CR1702), and *"Grandma"*(CR1703). All these legends have the motif of concealed dead bodies. The main difference is that in *"Grandma"* the discovery of the body would be by an unknown party (the thief), and the horrific find is left to your own imagination.

Final Thoughts

A version of this tale can be found at the Italian website "*http://leggende.clab.it*". The website has a section written in English which contains abstracts from different volumes of "*Tuttestorie Magazine*". This particular tale in question was written by Lucia Veccia, and is titled "*A Hearty Meal Into Ex-Jugoslavia*". The website is well worth a visit, although the English translation is a bit dodgy at times. But who am I to complain, I can't even order a cappuccino without getting it wrong!

PROJECT 2067

```
NAME:     The Beast of Belgium
CODE:     AW1908
ORIGIN:   1973, the author Joe Musser
STATUS:   False
```

The Beast Of Belgium

The rumour is that the EC has constructed a top-secret giant super computer based in Belgium, that contains databases full of information on every individual in the world. This giant computer is three stories high and occupies an unknown building in a Belgium city. The computer is solely self-programming, and is used to track every man, woman, and child on this planet.

The computer is seen as work by the anti-Christ, and will be used with the mark of the beast to control the global economy. It is this sinister motive that has earned the super computer the nickname of the "Beast".

Summary

This amazing but unbelievable rumour has dominated Christian circles for the last 30 years. The combination of the Christian beliefs of "the mark of the beast" mixed with the modern conspiracy theorists theory that a secret global government controls the world economy, makes a fascinating fusion of a legend that will not lie down and die.

The idea of a giant super computer that is three stories high was probably more believable when the legend first started back in 1973, but simply doesn't wash in today's silicone world of modern technology. We all know that with the capabilities of modern powerful computers, you wouldn't need a computer of that size to do the task. But as unbelievable as it is, this legend will keep being retold time and time again.

Another flaw is that the computer is supposed to be self-programming. There has been major advances in AI (Artificial Intelligence) over the last few years, but as far as I am aware it hasn't reached the "Antichrist" status just yet, so the idea of that kind of technology being around in the 1970's is just a joke. Even if the technology was available, how can you possibly track every human being on the planet?

No, as I have said, the "Belgium Beast " is a complete work of fiction. The legend was first recognised on a large scale when the magazine "Christian Life" printed the story in 1976. Soon after, "Christian Life" received a letter from Joe Musser who claimed he invented the story three years before hand. Apparently, the story was fabricated for his novel *Behold A Pale Horse* and the screenplay for the David Wilkerson film, *The Rapture*. Joe Musser was shocked that the story was taken as gospel (pardon the pun!) and stated that for three years he had watched the legend being passed around as fact.

The legend was hyped even more by the clever promotional campaign for the movie, *The Rapture*. Believable mock newspapers that featured the *Beast Of Belgium* story were printed and distributed, with hardly anything to suggest that the news stories printed were fiction.

Final Thoughts

Outside of Christian circles this legend would be scoffed immediately as a ridiculous conspiracy theory, but certain Christians have a deep seated mistrust and fear of new technology. This is nothing new, as through the ages Christians have often greeted technical advances as signs of *The Last Days*. T.V, Cinema, and pop music have all been greeted with suspicion, even being believed that they are the work of the antichrist. Some people believe that computers and the Internet are the tools that signify *The Last Days*, but not everybody is so fearful as many Christians use these channels to reach a broader audience and to spread the 'Word'.

PROJECT 2067

NAME: Cleaning Up With Toothpaste!
CODE: AW1909
ORIGIN: Holland
STATUS: False

Cleaning Up With Toothpaste

When an employee of a company barges into the Director's office and tells him that he has an excellent idea to generate a bigger profit, it had better be a good one…and this was! The company produced toothpaste, and the employee reckoned that he could boost sales by 10%. Intrigued, the Director asked how the employee proposes to achieve such a task.

Before the employee was willing to share his great idea, he made the Director sign an agreement that he has a right to a certain annual percentage of the profit (the percentage is unknown) for the rest of his life if the idea was used. This was all agreed, and the rest is history. The employee now lives a life of luxury, and is worth millions of pounds. So what was this great idea I hear you ask? Well, it's simple:

Enlarge the hole of the toothpaste tube by 10%. The consumers will not notice this change and put the same amount of toothpaste onto their toothbrushes. But because the hole is bigger, they will use more toothpaste and will have to buy new toothpaste tubes more regularly.

Summary

In the Netherlands, the term used for Urban Legends is *"Broodje aap verhalen"* which translates as *Monkey Burgers* in English. I collected this rags to riches tale from a Dutch website named *Monkey Burgers*, which was created by Patrick Arink.

Patrick has informed me that he first heard the legend being told in a pub in the early 90's (if the bloke down the pub told it, it must be true then!). Another time, he heard the story in a different part of the Netherlands while listening to a conversation on a bus.

As I have already stated, this is a typical modern rags to riches tale that most people can relate to as it rekindles the dream we all have of making it big. After all, if such a simple idea can bring success, why can't it happen to you?

It is also a success story for the small guy. What a great world we live in when low-level employees can out think the big corporate fat cats with their teams of advisers, high spending marketing strategies, and think tanks. There's hope for all of us!

Final Thoughts

As I have already said, the Dutch term for UL's translates as *Monkey Burgers* in English. I am sure I am not the only person to wonder why they are called Monkey Burgers, and I am sure I was not the last to think that it was probably the product of spending too much time in *those* Amsterdam cafes. Well, I have yet to have conformation on the meaning, but I do have a feeling that it originates from a legend that a certain fast food chain substituted beef for monkey meat in their burgers! If anyone has a clearer idea to the true meaning, please let me know.

If you are fluent in Dutch, you might want to visit Patrick Arink Dutch website. Naturally, being English, I cannot speak any other languages. Of course, I get by, by speaking LOUD and s l o w l y to foreigners!

PROJECT 2067

```
NAME:      Home Is Where The Airport Is
CODE:      AW1910
ORIGIN:    France
STATUS:    True
```

Home Is Where The Airport Is

A refugee from Iran has been stranded at the Charles De Gaulle Airport in Paris for well over a decade. Believe it or not, this is true!

Merhan Karimi Nasseri (nicknamed 'Sir Alfred' by airport staff) was expelled from Iran in 1977 for his vocal political views against the Shah of Iran. He quickly found himself with no home, passport, or documents, and with nowhere to go. Over the next few years Alfred desperately sought asylum in seven different European capitals to no avail, when in 1981, four years after he was deported from Iran, he was finally declared a political refugee by the United Nations High Commission in Belgium. With the vital documents he had waited so long to obtain, Alfred set out on his journey with a new revived enthusiasm. His destination? England.

He made it, but not for long, as fate dealt another cruel blow to his fortunes. After a long journey to Paris by train his briefcase was stolen at the railway station, and Alfred arrived in Paris without the important documents he was issued. Undeterred, Alfred went straight to the Charles De Gaulle Airport in Paris and boarded a plane for London. Customs staff at Heathrow airport did not greet him with open arms, and without any documents or a passport, they had no choice but to bundle him on the next plane back to Paris. To make the situation even worse (if it could get any worse!), the security at the Charles De Gaulle Airport arrested Alfred for illegal entry! The French wanted to deport him, but with no documents or a passport, they had nowhere to deport him to! Alfred spent the next few years in and out of jail for illegal immigration, before making Terminal One his adopted home.

A human rights lawyer took up the fight for Alfred's rights, but it took years for any progress to be made. Finally, in1992, a French court ruled that Alfred entered Terminal One as a political refugee and cannot be expelled from it. This was all very well, but the court could not force the French government to allow Alfred to leave the airport on French soil. The government refused to allow him citizenship in France, and wouldn't provide a transit visa.

Alfred needed to return to Belgium where he had received the original documents, but was unable to do so without a transit visa. The Belgium government were willing to hand Alfred the necessary documents, but he had to claim the papers in person! That's what I call a *catch 22* situation.

The legal battles continued, and in 1995 it looked as though Alfred's lawyer had made a breakthrough. Alfred was given permission to enter Belgium to regain his papers, but as always there was a catch! He was allowed to return only if he stayed in Belgium for a year under supervision by a social worker. Unbelievably, Alfred refused, claiming he would only leave Terminal One to travel to Britain.

Finally, in July 1999, Alfred was handed his papers by the Belgium government making Alfred a free man and allowing him to leave the airport any time he wished. But there is a final twist to the tale with a pinch of irony, as Alfred is still lodging at Terminal One. All those years stranded at the Airport must have made Alfred slightly *loco*, as he no longer wanted to leave. He feels safe in the boundaries of the terminal, and considers the airport staff as family.

'Sir Alfred' is still the resident celebrity of the Charles De Gaulle Airport, and receives many cards and letters from well-wishers from all over the world.

Summary

This amazingly true story is a great example of bureaucracy gone mad. No wonder the poor man has lost his marbles, he has had to endeavour years of slow legal battles and the mind blowing crazy procedures that doesn't seem to make any sense at all outside the world of law. The Belgium government claimed that they were sympathetic with *Sir Alfred's* situation, but claimed he had to come and claim the papers he needed in person, knowing full well that he was unable to leave the airport. Then we have the French who didn't want Alfred, but would not supply him with the transit visa he needed to leave the airport and travel to Belgium. This went on for years and years, proving what a crazy world we live in.

The only variation of detail from version to version of this fascinating true tale is the description of how he actually lost his papers in the first place. One article claims that he had sent the papers back to Belgium in a moment of "folly", while the Times claim that he lost the documents while on a ferry. Other articles claim that the documents were taken when he was mugged at a Paris train station, while most agree that the suitcase he was carrying that contained the papers were stolen on a train while Alfred was heading for Paris.

Alfred is now free to leave whenever he wishes, but to the best of my knowledge the airport still remains his home, why? Well, I guess it must be similar to prisoners that have spent a long term in jail. They have spent so long living in a routine and controlled environment, where they hardly have to think for themselves, they end up relying on the routine and would feel lost and isolated in the real world and unable to cope. The Charles De Gaulle is Alfred's prison, and has spent too long relying on the goodness of the hearts of the airport staff to fend for himself. He feels safe at the airport and probably would feel very vulnerable in the outside world.

Final Thoughts

I bet you are all wondering how Merhan Karimi Nasseri earned the nickname *Sir Alfred?* No! Well I am going to tell you anyway.

Alfred's quest to enter Britain never dwindled and he applied many times, each time getting turned down. On the immigration application forms there was a space to enter an adopted name of choice, Nasseri wrote Alfred in the box simply because he liked the name. Employees at the Charles De Gaulle Airport learned of this and started calling him *Sir Alfred* or just *Alfred*, and the name stuck.

AROUND THE WORLD

```
NAME:      Two Finger Salute
CODE:      AW1911
ORIGIN:    England (Battle of Agincourt)
STATUS:    True
```

Two Finger Salute

The two-finger salute is a universal gesture of defiance and anger used mainly in Britain. The reversed 'V' sign originated from the Battle of Agincourt in 1415, where the successful British soldiers used the sign as an act of defiance against the defeated French prisoners.

Before the battle the French anticipated victory, and threatened to cut off three fingers from the right hand of every man they captured. This would ensure that the famous English longbow archers would not be able to draw their bows and would be unable to fight again.

But against all odds, the English were victorious, and the two-fingered salute was given in a mocking fashion to all passing French prisoners to show that they still had all of their fingers.

Summary

Although widely used in Britain, the sign would not be recognised in many other countries throughout the world. It is similar in comparison to the American term of 'giving the finger', and is used in the same vein.

The origin theories of this fascinating legend are based on fact, but the actual battle of when the sign was first used has long been debated. Most agree that it was the Battle Of Agincourt in 1415, but another theory is Crecy in 1346. It almost certainly happened during the 'Hundred Years War' between England and France, which took place throughout the 14th and 15th centuries.

The *Battle Of Agincourt* took place when a battle weary English army led by Henry V were returning home from France after a long, and gruelling battle at Harfleur. The French blocked the English route to Calais, and so a battle was inevitable. The French were confident of victory, and were even laughing and joking over a big breakfast before the battle. The English were less confident and with good reason, the French army had 25,000 men, the English only 6,000.

Anticipating victory, the French bragged about how they were going to chop off three fingers from the right hand of every man they captured. This would ensure that the famous English Longbow Archers would never see battle again.

But against all odds the English were victorious. Apparently Henry V made a rousing speech just before the battle commenced, reminding the archers of the French threat of cutting off their fingers. This very thought must have driven their adrenalin through battle, and after victory they mocked the passing French prisoners by sticking up their two fingers to show that they still can draw a bow.

The rest is history.

Final Thoughts

Many claim the following to be true, but I seriously have my doubts! The bow used to be made from an English Yew tree, and the process of drawing the bow was known as "plucking the yew". So not only did the English stick their two fingers up to the French, but also, to let them know that they still can draw a bow, they shouted "pluck yew". Over the years the words have got distorted and the word "pluck" changed to the "F" word, with the whole meaning mutating into a sexual reference.

It is also said that the term "giving the bird" with reference to the one finger salute, is a symbolic gesture that originates from the fact that the arrows used contained pheasant feathers.

I don't know about you, but I think I will take that with a heavy dosage of salt!

NETLORE...

INTRODUCTION...PAGE 198

GOODTIMES...PAGE 201

BUDWEISER FROGS SCREENSAVER......................PAGE 204

RACIST WORD...PAGE 207

THE BROKEN CUP HOLDER.......................................PAGE 210

CRAIG SHERGOLD..PAGE 213

INTERNET CLEAN-UP DAY..PAGE 215

AIRCRAFT MAINTENANCE...PAGE 217

FOREIGN SIGNS...PAGE 219

PROJECT 2067

Thursday 18th, August
09:00: Arrived at the Office

CATEGORY: NETLORE

The cops have studied the building's CCTV footage from yesterday and have a clear picture of the man responsible for the break-in as he was leaving the premises. I have seen the picture of the suspected man and my mind is at rest because he is not a CIA or FBI agent, and he is not a member of the British Secret Service (perhaps my imagination was running a little too wild!), no, I instantly recognised him as Doug (pretty face) Moron. Doug is one of Angus Brute's cronies, and is instantly recognisable because he has a face that could strip paint from 50 yards. In fact, he is so ugly that the midwife slapped his mother when he was born. He is so ugly that back in London, a bulldog that is chewing a wasp is said to have a 'Chevy Chase' like Doug Moron! His bird is no oil painting either, her name is Sophie but all the lads call her Wendy because it looks like her face has been blown inside out.

That's enough of the ugly jokes; I have somehow wandered off the track. As I have said, Doug works for Brute, which means that Brute has got a whiff that I am onto something and is more than a little curious to what that could be. He probably thinks that it is some huge scandal like Madonna is secretly harbouring Michael Jackson's love child (she isn't!), and would probably be disappointed if he had found out the truth. I mean it isn't like my investigation will ruin anybody's lives; Brute prefers to drag a celebrity's name through the mud and then toss it on to the scrap heap before hyping up and knocking down his next victim. My investigation is to find the truths behind something that is more than just stories or idle gossip. These legends affect our everyday lives and sometimes attempt to control the way we think and I intend to find out why and how. The thought of this would be beyond Brute's comprehension. Not that it matters; Doug wouldn't have found anything as I had all my papers with me in my suitcase. Nevertheless, I will have to be more careful in the remaining days that I have got left.

The next category is Netlore, a relatively new subject in UL terms. Ever since skinny square-eyed nerds have been able to hack into top-secret military establishments or unleash a simple computer virus that has the capability to cripple half the world's economy, people are not only scared of this new technology, they are petrified, and who can blame them?

OK. So what has the Internet, James Bond and the space race got in common? They are all products of the cold war. It is hard to believe that the origins of the Internet started as a glimmer in the eyes of scientists' way back in the early 60's, and was first put into practice in 1969 when four US Universities were connected by ARPANET. The whole concept of the Internet was born from the US Government's fear of a nuclear attack by the Russians. If America did come under attack, there was a fear that the Government's communications network would be disabled and they would not be able to command their military. So in the case of such an emergency, the US government decided that information that needed to be sent to the military instantly by interconnecting certain positions across the country. Universities were the chosen positions and the Government funded the whole project.

In 1973 ARPANET had reached our shores, and connections between the University College in London and the Royal Radar Establishment in Norway was established. This was the first time that ARPANET had gone international.

Developments were continually made, and the massive boom of personal computers helped the growth of the Internet in the 1980's. With this new popularity came 'hackers', and a great concern over security and privacy arose. This worry was realised on Nov 1st 1988, when a program called 'Internet Worm' managed to disable 10% of the 60,000 Internet hosts.

The ARPANET was finally decommissioned in 1990, leading the way for a new and exiting project called the World Wide Web (WWW). Over the next few years saw the emergence of the first text based Web Sites and browsers. Major advances were made in the 1990's, helped by the creation of Gopher (the first point and click and menu way of navigation on the internet), Mosiac (the first browser), and the creation of HTML (Internet based language).

It is also important to mention that the origins of E-Mail were created by Ray Tomlinson way back in 1971, although this important discovery was hardly recognised at the time. So what was the first ever message sent from one computer to another I hear you ask? Well, it was probably 'QWERTYIOP', hardly the stuff for legend!

So there you have it, the Internet has emerged from the cold war with a military and research background, evolving into an 'information super highway' playing a major role in our everyday lives. But before the cyber world can start patting itself on the back it must realise that the silicon revolution has brought it's own dangers as baggage. Pornography is too easily accessible to kids and the Internet has acted as a springboard for the ever-increasing community of paedophiles. On-line banking and E-Commerce are most certainly the way forward, but the threat of security will always be its Achilles heel. The western world relies so heavily on this new technology that is possible for anyone with the means and knowledge to cripple governments and economies with a simple computer virus (e.g. The Love Letter). It is even possible for mass panic to be caused by clever hoaxes like the *Goodtimes virus* (NL6501), resulting in mass hysteria that any terrorist organisation would be proud of.

Fears and anxieties over modern technology have always been a favourite subject matter for folklorists to discuss, but the introduction of the Internet and E-Mails has forced in the new category Netlore. Netlore is folklore on speed. Instead of stories getting passed on by 'word of mouth' as in the traditional method they are spread through the use of E-Mail, reaching a global audience almost instantly. The Internet is the new medium for folklore, and this means that the term Netlore is not only used to describe the category, it is the name of this new medium for UL's.

NETLORE

NAME: Goodtimes Virus
CODE: NL6501
ORIGIN: 1994
STATUS: False

Goodtimes Virus: Version 1

```
Here is some important information. Beware of a file called
Goodtimes.

Happy Chanukah everyone, and be careful out there. There is a
virus on America Online being sent by E-Mail. If you get
anything called "Good Times", DON'T read it or download it. It
is a virus that will erase your hard drive. Forward this to all
your friends. It may help them a lot.
```

Goodtimes Virus: Version 2

```
Thought you might like to know...

Apparently, a new computer virus has been engineered by a user
of America Online that is unparalleled in its destructive
capability. Other, more well-known viruses such as Stoned,
Airwolf, and Michaelangelo pale in comparison to the prospects
of this newest creation by a warped mentality.What makes this
virus so terrifying is the fact that no program needs to be
exchanged for a new computer to be infected. It can be spread
through the existing e-mail systems of the Internet.

Luckily, there is one sure means of detecting what is now known
as the "Good Times" virus. It always travels to new computers
the same way - in a text e-mail message with the subject line
reading simply "Good Times". Avoiding infection is easy once the
file has been received - not reading it. The act of loading the
file into the mail server's ASCII buffer causes the "Good Times"
mainline program to initialise and execute.

The program is highly intelligent - it will send copies of
itself to everyone whose e-mail address is contained in a
received-mail file or a sent-mail file, if it can find one. It
will then proceed to trash the computer it is running on.
The bottom line here is - if you receive a file with the subject
line "Good Times", delete it immediately! Do not read it! Rest
assured that whoever's name was on the "From:" line was surely
struck by the virus. Warn your friends and local system users of
this newest threat to the Internet!
```

Summary

Goodtimes is the original computer virus hoax classic, and it sent mass panic across the English-speaking world when the original version was started back in December 1994.

The warnings claimed that by simply opening an E-Mail named *Goodtimes*, your computer would be infected by the virus and your whole Hard Drive would be wiped out. Experts were quick to denounce the virus as a hoax as it was not possible to execute a program just by simply opening an E-Mail. This did little to stem the panic, and large companies such as Citibank, Texas Instruments and AT&T fell for it hook, line, and sinker. Even American Government agencies were affected, such as the Department of Defence and NASA. The spread of the hoax has been blamed on business management personnel who did possess the knowledge to spot it as a hoax, but had the ability to spread the hoax on a wide scale very rapidly.

Version A is a copy of one of the original E-Mail messages that were sent out in 1994. As you can see, the original was short, sweet and to the point. You will also notice that the season greeting "Happy Chanukah" is also included in the warning. "Chanukah" is the Jewish holiday for the festival of lights, and this dates the E-Mail to early December, late November.

Version B is a latter version, and probably the version most commonly found. The message is a lot more long winded and goes into greater detail on the technicality of the virus.

Both versions of the hoax shown above are replicates of the original copies, and the spelling and grammar mistakes have been left untouched. Just thought I would let you know in case you thought that they were my mistakes!

No one knows for sure who actually started the hoax, and probably never will. The date most commonly associated with the original Goodtimes virus is December 2, 1994. One copy was found with the date being 29th November, 1994. Although this date could have easily been forged.

Final Thoughts

A computer virus is a patch or snippet of computer code that first infects the host program, and then starts to perform its task. The virus usually corrupts the program into performing other tasks that result in the virus being spread to other programs. Viruses are usually spread to other computers by infected programs on floppy discs, CD ROMs, or on attachment programs by E-Mail.

You could say that the hoax itself is a virus, the same way that UL's are. The hoaxes are spread rapidly via E-Mails and can cause as much panic and paranoia as real viruses. Instead of a snippet of code infecting a computer and making it perform tasks, the hoax manipulates the reader into sending out other hoax warning E-Mails. So you could say that the hoax, like a computer virus, is self-replicating.

PROJECT 2067

NAME: Budweiser Frogs Screensaver
CODE: NL6502
ORIGIN: 1997
STATUS: False

Budweiser Frogs Screensaver: Version 1

```
DANGER! VIRUS ALERT!
====================
THIS IS A NEW TWIST. SOME CREEPOID SCAM-ARTIST IS SENDING OUT A
VERY DESIRABLE SCREEN-SAVER {{THE BUD FROGS}}. IF YOU DOWN-LOAD
IT, YOU'LL LOSE EVERYTHING!!!! YOUR HARD DRIVE WILL CRASH!!
DON'T DOWNLOAD THIS UNDER ANY CIRCUMSTANCES!!! IT WENT INTO
CIRCULATION ON 13/05/97
PLEASE DISTRIBUTE THIS WARNING TO AS MANY PEOPLE AS POSSIBLE...
BELOW IS WHAT THE SCREENSAVER PROGGIE WOULD LOOK LIKE!
File: BUDSAVER.EXE (24643 bytes)
DL Time (28800 bps): < 1 minute
```

Budweiser Frogs Screensaver: Version 2

```
I have received a warning from a v.reliable source
regarding an EVIL new virus.

PLEASE NOTE:
You may receive an Email from an apparently harmless Budweiser
screen saver, entitled BUDDYLST.SIP
If you do, DO NOT OPEN IT UNDER ANY CIRCUMSTANCES!
Once opened, you will lose EVERYTHING on your PC. Your
hard disk will be completely destroyed and the person who
sent you the message will have access to your name and
password via the Internet. As far as we know this virus
was circulated yesterday morning. It's a brand new virus
and extremely dangerous.

Please copy this information and Email it to everyone in
your address book. We need to do all we can to block this
virus. AOL, Demon and now BT Internet have confirmed how
dangerous it is and there is no Anti-Virus program as yet
capable of destroying it. Please take all necessary
precautions and pass this information on to your friends,
acquaintances and work colleagues.
```

Summary

Long before "WASSUPP" was shouted down phones at every opportunity, Budweiser had a successful marketing campaign with the Budweiser frogs. The unlikely reptile stars were an instant success, and in 1996, a free downloadable screensaver of the "Bud Frogs" from Budweiser proved to be popular. But of course, there is always someone who has to try and spoil it for everyone!

In 1997, with the free download growing ever more popular, some prankster (or a word to that effect!) decided to try and burst Budweiser's bubble with a virus hoax.
The hoax was spread like wild fire via E-Mail, and was a little more harder to spot as a hoax than it's predecessors as it claimed that the virus was contained in the executable file, rather than the actual text of the E-Mail (which cannot be done).

Version 1 is a copy of one of the earliest versions that were being sent out in 1997. The warning is short and very primitive. The amount of exclamation points used to over state a point made it easy pickings for hoax-busters.

Version 2 is a later version and like so many others has an extra twist. Not only will your hard drive be wiped, but also the person who sent you the virus would have access to your name and password via the Internet. *Version 2* is a little more complex, and so maybe a little more believable than *Version 1*.

Of course, needless to say that the both versions shown are copies of the original hoaxes that plagued good peoples inbox's, and so the spelling and grammar has been left untouched.

Final Thoughts

Computer virus hoaxes are a real menace and can achieve as much damage as a real virus. They may not wipe your hard drive, but the physiological effects can be devastating. The fear of a virus causes a loss of confidence and bad publicity, and this vicious circle can hit companies and people hard.

There are loads of anti-virus websites on the Internet that can inform you whether a virus warning is real or just a hoax. These websites advise that the best way to stamp out a virus hoax is to have a better awareness and simply not to forward on the warnings. If only it was that simple!

PROJECT 2067

Please be careful when opening any executable file contained within E-Mail, especially if you don't know the person who sent it.

NETLORE

```
NAME:      Racist Word
CODE:      NL6503
ORIGIN:    Unknown
STATUS:    False
```

Racist Word

It is claimed that Microsoft are part of a global racist conspiracy spreading its messages of hate throughout the world. The proof has not been discovered in a piece of complex programming by a sophisticated hacker, in fact it hasn't been hidden at all and can easily be accessed by anyone. The proof can be found in the Thesaurus function of MS Word.

Type the following sentence in MS Word and highlight it:

"I hope Microsoft will rule the World."

Now enter the Thesaurus function and you will see:

"I should say so"

It gets worse! Now type in:

"I'd like all gays dead."

The Thesaurus responds:

"I'll drink to that"

And if that wasn't bad enough, type in:

"Kill all Jews."

The response is:

"Kill in cold blood"

If you have MS Word on your computer, try this, and discover the horrifying truth.

Summary

This piece of Netlore is one of many that can be categorised as part of the growing "Anti Bill Gates" society, and there are plenty of those who are opposed to the geek turned good. Bill Gates is the focus of a barrage of legends that either targets him personally or his Microsoft Company. Bill Gates has been accused of everything from being an anti-semitic devil worshipper; to being part of a global conspiracy conspiring to rule the world and spread it's messages of hate. A bit dramatic, maybe, but it shows the depth of hate that people harbour and the lengths that they will go to to tarnish the name of one of the richest men in the world.

So, is there any truth in the claim that the Thesaurus in MS Word is proof of all these wild allegations? Well, I tried these sentences out on my trusty version of Word and the thesaurus certainly didn't come out with the alleged comments. Although this does not mean that earlier versions didn't, and the language setting may have to be in US English.

When I typed in "I hope Microsoft rules the world", my thesaurus came up with "I imagine" which could be seen as a similar response, but when I looked down the list I also found "ill-advised", which is contradictory to the theory.

I then typed in the sentence "I'd like all gays dead", and one of the responses of the MS Word Thesaurus was "Idolize", but another response was "I don't know". With the sentence "Kill all Jews", one of the responses was "Kill in cold blood"!

It is easy to manipulate a Thesaurus list for your own purposes when looking up a word or phrase. Using one phrase or word from the list is really using circumstantial and selective evidence, and therefore cannot be used as verified proof. In fact, all the Thesaurus is doing is returning everyday words and expressions in alphabetical order. In fact, instead of inserting "I hope Microsoft rules the world", you could insert "I hope Bill Gates eats dung for breakfast" and the Thesaurus response would be exactly the same. So as you can see, there is nothing sinister about it at all!

Although the Thesaurus responses of the above contain no intentional ill feelings, the same cannot be said when Microsoft contracted out the programming of Windows 95 for the Chinese market. A few Taiwan Chinese programmers took this as a chance to spread their political hatred of the Chinese leaders to the whole of the Chinese market, and inserted such phrases as calling the Beijing leaders "Communist Bandits". Other suggestions to finish sentences urged loyal Taiwanese to "take to the mainland". Microsoft quickly realised what had been done and promptly removed all the offensive phrases from the system, and so avoiding a diplomatic crisis.

Final Thoughts

As an experiment I typed in the same sentence "I hope Microsoft will rule the world" onto a Lotus WordPro document (a rival of Microsoft), and checked out the thesaurus for the response. The result was quite surprising but blatantly honest, the response was "I think not" and "I don't think so". I am sure that's just a coincidence, don't you?

PROJECT 2067

```
NAME:      The Broken Cup holder
CODE:      NL6504
ORIGIN:    1996
STATUS:    True
```

The Broken Cup holder: Version 1

The following conversation took place at a technical support centre for computer users based in England:

Technician: Hello, this is technical support, how may I help you?

Caller: Hello, can you help me? The cup holder on the front of my computer has broken off.

Technician: Did you say cup holder?

Caller: Yes, the little tray to put your drinks on that slides out from the front of the computer has broken off.

Technician: Was the cup holder installed when you bought the computer, or has it been a customised addition since?

Caller: It came with the computer. The name on the front is 4X.

At this point the technician bursts out laughing as he realises that the cup holder is actually the CD ROM player!

The Broken Cup Holder: Version 2

True story from a Novell NetWare SysOp:

Caller: "Hello, is this Tech Support?"

Tech Rep: " Yes, it is. How may I help you?"

Caller: "The cup holder on my PC is broken and I am within my warranty period. How do I go about getting that fixed?"

NETLORE

Tech Rep: "I'm sorry, but did you say a cup holder?"

Caller: "Yes, it's attached to the front of my computer."

Tech Rep: " Please excuse me if I seem a bit stumped, it's because I am. Did you receive this as part of a promotional, at a trade show? How did you get this cup holder? Does it have a trade mark?"

Caller: "It came with my computer, I don't know anything about a promotion. It just has '4X' on it."

At this point the Tech Rep had to mute the caller, because he couldn't stand it. The caller had been using the load drawer of the CD - ROM drive as a cup holder, and had snapped it off the drive.

Summary

Yes, I know, believe it or not there really are people out there who are that stupid! There are many tech support stories, but this one is probably the most famous. Although this is widely stated as being a true incident, I have yet to see any verification of the authenticity of the legend. The later versions (such as *Version 1*) are normally stated as to have happened in England, but Company names are not normally stated. Only in the early versions (such as *Version 2*) are the names of the companies included, and they are usually large computer companies such as Apple or Novell Netware. The origins of the story are unclear, but *Version 2* is the earliest I have found, and it is a copy of an E-mail that was sent on the 19th June 1996.

The Broken Cupholder legend proves that some people's fear of new technology is completely justified! Not everyone's lift stops at the top floor (if you know what I mean?), and some people should just stick to a typewriter.

Final Thoughts

As I have already stated, there are plenty of Tech Support legends travelling the E-Mail circuit, and one of my favourites is a recorded message left on an answer machine. This bloke claims that his "pointer" is in the middle of the screen and is unable to move it left because his mouse is on the left edge of the pad, and if he moves it any more the mouse will go off the pad! Enough said.

PROJECT 2067

NAME: Craig Shergold
CODE: NL6505
ORIGIN: 13th February, 1989
STATUS: True

Craig Shergold

Craig Shergold is a seven-year-old boy from Carlshalton, Surrey, who is dying from an inoperable brain tumour. It is his wish to enter the Guinness Book of Records for the largest amount of 'get well' cards received by one person.

Please find it in your heart to spare a moment of your time to help fulfil Craig's wish.

Please send your card to the following address:

Craig Shergold
38 Shelby Road
Carshalton
Surrey

P.S. Please pass this message on to all your friends and relatives

Summary

Although the legend of Craig Shergold is extremely well padded around the edges, it is based on a true story. The truth is that Craig Shergold was actually a 9-year-old boy when he was diagnosed with cancer (following a brain tumour) on the 13th February 1989. Craig received many get-well cards from friends and relatives, and it was his doctor's idea to campaign for the Guinness Book of Records. At that stage Craig had only received 200 cards, but after his plight had reached headline news in the Mirror and the Sun, the cards were soon pouring in. It is estimated that by October 1989, 200,000 cards a week were being sent. This was a major problem as the special sorting room set up at Sutton United Football club, could only handle about 60,000 a week.

The record to beat stood at just over a million cards, and a boy named Mario Morby from Leicester held that record. On the 16th November 1989, Mario's record had been smashed, and still the cards kept piling in for Craig.

NETLORE

In 1991, American billionaire John W Kluge flew Craig to the University of Virginia Medical Centre for an operation to remove the benign brain tumour. After the successful operation, Craig and his family thanked everyone who had sent Craig a card but appealed for no more cards to be sent so that they could live a normal life. Mainly thanks to chain E-Mails the appeal was in vain, and the cards just kept pouring in. One source has roughly estimated that Craig has received over a hundred million cards. I am surprised that Clinton Cards did not open up a special 'Get Well Craig' section in their shops!

Of course, with legends the facts can get a little blurred around the edges, and the *Craig Shergold* legend is no exception. Craig's surname has also been Sherwood, Sherhold, Shargold, and shirgold. The county of Surrey has been changed to Surry, or Surney. Carshalton is also known as Charshalton, Carshaltonn or Carshelton. Some chain letters even claim that Craig lives in Canada or Virginia, USA.

Final Thoughts

The heart-warming story of Craig Shergold has long been obscured by legend, and the results have been damaging, wasting time and resources for charities and organisations for the needy. The latest chain letters urge readers to forward their cards to the "Make-A-Wish Foundation', Virginia, Georgia. The foundation has had to add a page debunking such legends on their Web site. They state that all cards received for Craig Shergold will be forwarded straight to a recycling centre.

PROJECT 2067

NAME: Internet Clean-Up Day
CODE: NL6506
ORIGIN: 1996
STATUS: False

Internet Clean-Up Day

```
Subj: Internet Cleanup Day

THIS MESSAGE WILL AGAIN BE REPEATED IN MID FEBRUARY.

*** Attention ***

It's that time again!

As many of you know, each year the Internet must be shut down
for 24 hours in order to allow us to clean it. The cleaning
process, which eliminates dead email and inactive ftp, www and
gopher sites, allows for a better working and faster Internet.

This year, the cleaning process will take place from 12:01 a.m.
GMT on February 27 until 12:01 a.m. GMT on February 28 (the time
least likely to interfere with ongoing work). During that 24-
hour period, five powerful Internet search engines situated
around the world will search the Internet and delete any data
that they find.

In order to protect your valuable data from deletion we ask that
you do the following:

Disconnect all terminals and local area networks from their
Internet connections.
Shut down all Internet servers, or disconnect them from the
Internet.
Disconnect all disks and hard drives from any connections to the
Internet.
Refrain from connecting any computer to the Internet in any way.
We understand the inconvenience that this may cause some
Internet users, and we apologize. However, we are certain that
any inconveniences will be more than made up for by the
increased speed and efficiency of the Internet, once it has been
cleared of electronic flotsam and jetsam.

We thank you for your cooperation.

***** Signature Removed *****
```

Summary

This version is a direct copy of an E-Mail circular, and early versions of the *Internet Clean-Up Day* started circulating in 1996. Since then, it has become a yearly April Fools joke, and a legend in it's own right. The annual hoax usually claims to be a public service announcement, and states that on a certain day the Internet will be cleaned of all junk mail, bookmarks and unused files. In doing so, the Internet will become faster and more efficient.

Final Thoughts

Most versions ask you to turn off the computer and disconnect any links to the Internet, but one version stated that all you had to do was to put a cloth over the computer for the day!

Even though this hoax reappears year after year, there are still people out there stupid enough to fall for it. There is NO Internet clean-up day, and the Internet will still be as slow as ever!

PROJECT 2067

NAME: Aircraft Maintenance
CODE: NL6507
ORIGIN: Unknown
STATUS: Undecided

Aircraft Maintenance

After every flight, pilots complete a gripe sheet which conveys to the mechanical problems encountered with the aircraft during the flight that need repair or correction.

The form is a piece of paper that the pilot completes and then the mechanics read and correct the problem. They then respond in writing on the lower half of the form what remedial action was taken and the pilot reviews the gripe sheets before the next flight.

Here are some actual logged maintenance complaints and problems,

  P = The problem logged by the pilot.
  S = The solution and action taken by the engineers.

  P: Left inside main tyre almost needs replacement.
  S: Almost replaced left inside main tyre.

  P: Test flight OK, except autoland very rough.
  S: Autoland not installed on this aircraft.

  P: Something loose in cockpit.
  S: Something tightened in cockpit.

  P: Dead bugs on windshield.
  S: Live bugs on back-order.

  P: Autopilot in altitude-hold mode produces a 200 fpm descent.
  S: Cannot reproduce problem on ground.

  P: Evidence of leak on right main landing gear.
  S: Evidence removed.

  P: DME volume unbelievably loud.
  S: DME volume set to more believable level.

  P: Aircraft handles funny.
  S: Aircraft warned to straighten up, fly right, and be serious

NETLORE

Summary

This is a copy of an E-Mail that I had received in October 2002. The spelling and grammar was so bad in the original that I had to make a few corrections in order for it to be comprehensible, other than that, it is in the original wording.

This "list" arrangement is an instantly recognisable format in UL circles, and is used to document everything from computer helpline conversations, doctor's notes on patients, quotes from the courtroom, excuses from parents for students, quotes from accident report forms, to signs and menus translated into poor English by foreigners. I could go on and on reeling off the categories, and could easily have enough material for a large book.

Most of this material that is circulated via E-Mails today could have been found sitting on top of a Fax machine's in-tray ten years ago. This in turn could have been found pinned up on company's bulletin board or printed in a newsletter 30 to 40 years before that. In other words, this is a typical "office water cooler conversation" that reproduces and recycles the same information but with variations. This is why I consider the "lists" as UL's.

Final Thoughts

Here are a few examples of "List" legends:

Absent notes for students from their parents:
Please excuse Fiona from being absent yesterday. She was in bed with Gramps.
My son is under the doctor's care and should not take PE. Please execute him.

Doctors Notes:
The patient refused an autopsy.
The patient has no past history of suicides.
She is numb from her toes down.

Lawyer's questions in court:

Was that the same nose you broke as a child?
How long have you been a French Canadian?
Was it you or your brother who was killed in the war?

PROJECT 2067

NAME: Foreign Signs
CODE: NL6508
ORIGIN: Unknown
STATUS: Undecided

Foreign Signs

The following signs have been found in various locations, using the English language somewhat creatively...

At a Budapest zoo:
PLEASE DO NOT FEED THE ANIMALS. IF YOU HAVE ANY SUITABLE FOOD, GIVE IT TO THE GUARD ON DUTY.

Doctor's office, Rome:
SPECIALIST IN WOMEN AND OTHER DISEASES.

Hotel, Acapulco:
THE MANAGER HAS PERSONALLY PASSED ALL THE WATER SERVED HERE.

Sign in men's rest room in Japan:
TO STOP LEAK TURN COCK TO THE RIGHT

In a City restaurant:
OPEN SEVEN DAYS A WEEK, AND WEEKENDS TOO.

A sign seen on an automatic restroom hand dryer:
DO NOT ACTIVATE WITH WET HANDS.

In a Pumwani maternity ward:
NO CHILDREN ALLOWED.

Sign in Japanese public bath:
FOREIGN GUESTS ARE REQUESTED NOT TO PULL COCK IN TUB.

Tokyo hotel's rules and regulations:
GUESTS ARE REQUESTED NOT TO SMOKE OR DO OTHER DISGUSTING BEHAVIOURS IN BED.

In a Tokyo bar:
SPECIAL COCKTAILS FOR THE LADIES WITH NUTS.

In a Bangkok temple:
IT IS FORBIDDEN TO ENTER A WOMAN EVEN A FOREIGNER IF DRESSED AS A MAN.

NETLORE

```
Hotel, Japan:
YOU ARE INVITED TO TAKE ADVANTAGE OF THE CHAMBERMAID.

Airline ticket office, Copenhagen:
WE TAKE YOUR BAGS AND SEND THEM IN ALL DIRECTIONS.
```

Summary

This is the complete copy of an E-Mail that I received on the 13th December 2001, and is a good example of many that I have received over the last few years. Foreign interpretation of the English language has always given much amusement to the English-speaking world. English is a dominant language in the world, so other languages are often translated into English on signs, menus, etc. A bad grasp of this complex language can cause some very humorous translations.

'List' legends have already been discussed in *Aircraft Maintenance* (NL6507), and 'Foreign Signs' is a huge bulk of a category within that format.

Final Thoughts

Of course, the importance of understanding the language you wish to communicate with can work both ways, as Nike found out to their embarrassment. You may recall a Nike advert with Samburu tribesmen crossing Kenya, with one of the tribe at the end speaking his native language and the subtitle at the bottom of the screen reads, "Just Do It!"

But the tribesman was not as happy with his trainers as everyone thought, because what he actually said was, "I don't want these. Give me big shoes!"

This was not noticed until a couple of weeks into the advertising campaign. Then, to Nikes great embarrassment, the mistake was plastered across every national American Newspaper. Some may say that this is another great example of a large corporate company not caring to pay attention to detail and ending up with egg on their face. A little research was all that was needed, and if they thought that no one in their audience would notice a mistake is just stupid. Within the large and multi-cultured society that is America, someone was bound to speak the Maa language.

9\11...

INTRODUCTION	PAGE 222
BERT IS EVIL	PAGE 224
WINGDINGS CONSPIRACY	PAGE 226
THE NOSTRADAMUS PREDICTIONS	PAGE 229
THE STARBUCKS OUTRAGE	PAGE 232
THE $20 PREDICTION	PAGE 234
IT'S A LOTTERY	PAGE 236
THE PENTAGON ATTACK	PAGE 238
THE BIRMINGHAM WARNING	PAGE 243
JACKIE CHAN'S LUCKY ESCAPE	PAGE 246
THE COKE WARNING	PAGE 248
THE DEVIL'S FACE IN THE SMOKE	PAGE 250

PROJECT 2067

Thursday 18th, August
13:00: Library

CATEGORY: 9/11

In my introduction I wrote of the mystic skyline of New York City, but of course
the events of September 11th 2001 have fatefully changed that skyline forever.
When the Al Queda terrorists decided to use human bombs to cause maximum
damage and fatalities, a new evil of global terrorism was brought onto the world
stage. Out of the smouldering smoke of 'Ground Zero' a new era was dawning,
and the world will never be the same again. 9/11 affected many people from
different countries and religions, and these callous acts of evil sent out a cold
shiver that stretched across to the four corners of the earth. World views and
politics have, and will be, reshaped forever. The prospects are frightening, and
no one quite knows where the war on terror will take us. One thing is for sure,
ways of combating terrorism will be relentlessly pursued, and this will include
everything from freezing their finances to targeting countries that harbour them.
These are truly turbulent times and a black mark on the pages of history.

It came as no surprise that in one of the bleakest hours of modern history, UL's
poured out of the gaping wound like a swarm of locus. The fact that the focus of
these legends are on 9/11 offend and appal many people and can be viewed as
disrespectful and insensitive, but, like jokes, these legends can be seen as part of a
healing process in the wake of a tragedy. These legends contain controversy,
conspiracies, humour, and sinister predictions, all of which are a formula to try
and make sense of a situation that most of us simply cannot comprehend.

The ULs surrounding the events of 9/11 form a very important reflection of the
fears and thoughts that capture the aftermath of the tragedy. They are also
being used as a propaganda tool in the fight against terrorism, mirroring the use
of UL's in any war.

It would be impossible to include all the UL's surrounding the events of 9/11 as
it would take a huge book to cover half of the legends, and new ones are
surfacing on a daily basis. Some of the ULs out there are in bad taste and I have
been very selective of the ones to which I have included in this chapter.

The most controversial UL I have tackled in this category has to be *Pentagon
Attack* (WT9807). This conspiracy theory asks questions about the official
version given that an aircraft crashed into the Pentagon on 9/11. I have

222

investigated each one of the questions in turn and reported the findings. Don't try and read this one last thing at night!

The Birmingham Warning (WT9808) deals with a subject much closer to home, while you computer club nerds will know all about the *Wingdings Conspiracy* (WT9802). Bill Gates again-give the bloke a break!

After any tragic event people wonder what they could have done to prevent it. Some seek refuge in the theory that it was 'fate' and it was 'meant to be'. This line of thinking is often backed up by prediction theories. In the aftermath of 9/11 many of these theories emerged, ranging from a prediction in a $20 note (WT9805) to the old favourite Nostradamus (WT9803), who has apparently predicted everything from the Great Fire Of London, both World Wars, to the eerie prediction that I will have scrambled eggs for my breakfast next Thursday!

And for those of you that have fond memories of the children's TV favourite Sesame Street, you will be horrified to hear that Bert has been linked to Osama Bin Laden. You don't believe me? Check out *Bert Is Evil* (WT9801), and you will see what I mean.

As I have said, I have been very selective in the choice of material to include for 9/11, and I will now leave you to form your own opinions and thoughts of these legends. I am currently in the library carrying out vital research for the project, and will probably be here all afternoon as I have a lot to do.

There are certain events in history that get engraved in the memory of many people throughout the world. People say that they will always remember what they were doing the exact moment that they had heard that JFK had been shot, when man first landed on the moon, or when Princess Diana tragically died in a car accident. You will probably always remember what you were doing when the events unfolded on the fateful day of 11th September 2001.

PROJECT 2067

```
NAME:     Bert is Evil
CODE:     WT9801
ORIGIN:   October, 2001
STATUS:   True
```

Bert is Evil

Sesame Street's Bert can be seen peering over the shoulder of Osama Bin Laden in posters used by Al Queda supporters in Afghanistan, protesting against American led attacks on the Taliban regime.

Summary

Remarkably this is true, the familiar face of lovable Bert can be seen side by side with the world's most notorious terrorist leader, Osama Bin Laden. So, *how* exactly did this happen?

First of all I need to explain the whole *Bert is Evil* thing. It was all started by a man named Dino Ignacio, who started his humorous website as part of a long running joke claiming that Bert is evil. To prove this, Bert was inserted side by side with the world's most notorious evil figures throughout history. The *Bert is evil* Website reached cult status with many mirror sites being started up.

OK, so we know the origins of why there is a photo of Osama Bin Laden shoulder to shoulder with Bert, but how did it get printed on protester posters in Bangladesh? Mostafa Kamal, the production manager of Azad Products who made the posters, reveals the answer. Apparently he found the image on the Internet and included the image on the 2,000 posters he printed, not realising that Bert was there! Mostafa stated that he would not include the image on the next poster design.

Shortly after the Bert and Bin Laden image was used on the protesters posters, Dino Ignacio closed the official *Bert is Evil* website. Dino claimed that the cult had grown too big and too close to reality. *Bert is Evil* had become too commercialised and had achieved a much greater platform of awareness than Dino had wanted. In other words, it had become more than just a joke. Dino claims that Sesame St. played a major part in his childhood, and now that the *Bert is Evil* cult had reached the mass media, he didn't wish to have any part in damaging the image of Bert for the children. Dino has appealed to all the mirror sites to follow suit.

Final Thoughts

The photographs of the poster at anti US rallies were printed in newspapers throughout the world, and many theories of why the Bert image was inserted on the posters were circulating. One theory was that the CIA had secretly sabotaged the posters design by inserting the image of Bert next to Osama Bin Laden. The aim of this propaganda coup was to mock the Taliban by using Bert as a symbol of western commercialism and freedom.

By using the code you can view the picture of the poster by visiting the Project 2067 website at:

www.project2067.com

PROJECT 2067

```
NAME:      Wingdings Conspiracy
CODE:      WT9802
ORIGIN:    1992
STATUS:    False
```

Wingdings Conspiracy   Example 1

Follow the instructions below to uncover a sinister conspiracy involving the Wingdings font that may suggest some kind of link between Microsoft and 09\11.

1. First type the following in capital letters "NYC" (short for New York City).

2. Highlight the text and change the size to 72.

3. Highlight and change the font to "Webdings" – the results are interesting!

4. Now change the font to "Wingdings" – even more interesting!!

Wingdings Conspiracy   Example 2

The flight number of one of the planes that flew into the World Trade Centre was Q33NY.

1. Open a new Word document and type "Q33NY" in capital letters

2. Highlight the text and enlarge the text to size "48"

3. Change the Font style to "Wingdings"

You will be amazed!!

9/11

Summary

First of all, for those with the means to do so, I recommend that you actually try the above examples for yourselves. For the rest of you, here is what all the fuss is about:

NYC in "Webdings":

NYC in "Wingdings":

Q33NY in "Wingdings"

The "Wingdings" and the "Webdings" fonts are designed to illustrate graphic icons instead of letters. "Wingdings" has been around a lot longer than "Webdings", and first had the conspiracy theorists wetting their pants in 1992 with the "NYC" hidden meaning. Back then Microsoft were being accused of being anti-semitism, with the sign being interpreted as "Death to all Jews". With the skull and crossbones representing death with the Star of David representing Jews, the theory was sort of plausible and even had the New York Post giving it headline news. Microsoft denied all the allegations and put the *secret message* down to nothing but a coincidence.

Since the events of 9/11 the *secret message* is seen as a prediction and has taken on a completely different meaning, with the emphasis being on the terrorist attacks on New York City on the fateful day on September 11th 2001.

The "Webdings" version of NYC is probably less of a coincidence, and probably was devised to mock the conspiracy theorists that had too much time on their hands and were bound to seek more *hidden meanings*. The webdings version can be interpreted as "I Love New York". Look at the example above and you will see what I mean.

Finally, we will look at the eerie interpretation of flight Q33NY, which according to the E-Mails is the flight number of one of the planes that crashed into the World Trade centre. With a little imagination (the two pieces of paper being the two towers!) the Wingdings images certainly portray the scene to that particular act of terrorism. That is apart from one major flaw; there was no such flight number as Q33NY. The actual flight numbers of the two aircrafts that crashed into the World Trade Centre are American Airlines Flight 11, and United Airlines Flight 175. No eerie prediction here, just good old fashioned bending of the truth!

Final Thoughts

With the entire phobia surrounding the Millennium, in 1999 a new wingdings prophetic theory was born. Worries over the Millennium bug (computers unable to cope with the date format) and hype over the Nostradamus predictions (not to mention Prince!), 1999 was a turbulent time and people were literally heading for the hills. Perfect ground for UL's, and they didn't disappoint. It was pointed out that MILLENIUM in the wingdings font translates to the following:

In 1999, this was seen as a prediction and therefore pretty scary stuff, which heightened the fears and hype that shrouded the turn of the Millennium. Of course, NOTHING happened (apart from many hangovers that is!).

```
NAME:     The Nostradamus Predictions
CODE:     WT9803
ORIGIN:   September 11th, 2001
STATUS:   False
```

The Nostradamus Predictions: Example 1

"In the year of the new century and nine months,
From the sky will come a great King of Terror...
The sky will burn at forty-five degrees.
Fire approaches the great new city..."

"In the city of York there will be a great collapse,
2 twin brothers torn apart by chaos
While the fortress falls the great leader will succumb
Third big war will begin when the big city is burning"

- NOSTRADAMUS

The Nostradamus Predictions: Example 2

Subject: Re: Nostradamus

Century 6, Quatrain 97

Two steel birds will fall from the sky on the
Metropolis. The sky will burn at forty-five degrees
latitude. (*New York City lies between 40-45 degrees*)
Fire approaches the great new city

 Immediately a huge, scattered flame leaps up. Within months,
rivers will flow with blood. The undead will roam
Earth for little time.

The Nostradamus Predictions: Example 3

"In the City of God there will be a great thunder,

Two brothers torn apart by Chaos, while the fortress endures, the great leader will succumb",
The third big war will begin when the big city is burning"

- Nostradamus 1654

Summary

Did Nostradamus actually predict the terrorist atrocities on New York City on 11th September 2001? The simple answer is no! For those of you who do not know who the hell Nostradamus is (shame on you), I will give a brief lesson in history before continuing. Nostradamus was a French astrologer born in 1503, and is credited for predicting everything from the Great Fire Of London, The Great Plague, the rise and fall of Adolf Hitler, WW2, and ultimately it is widely believed that he has predicted the end of the world! Most of these predictions have come from a collection of prophecies published in 1555 called the Centuries, and each prediction is told in a separate four line rhyming verse called a quatrain. The predictions are very vague and are usually open for interpretation, and therefore misinterpretation. It is believed that Nostradamus relied heavily on Occult divination and horoscopes to enter deep trances that led to his predictions; this led to his prophecies being condemned by the Catholic Church Congregation in 1781. Although his prophecies have caused much controversy and has caught the imagination of many over the years, he was also know as a pioneer in alternative medicines and treatment for the plague outbreak in 1546-47. History lesson finished.

Example 1 is one of the most common and believable out of all the variations. The only problem is that Nostradamus, like all the other versions, never actually made this prediction. Instead, it has been made up of snippets of different quatrains and pieced together like a jigsaw. In one quatrain Nostradamus did actually write that "The sky will burn at forty-five degrees latitude, Fire approaches the new city". New York is positioned between forty and forty one degrees latitude, and not at 45 as it has been claimed. Some may argue that the forty-five could actually mean 40.5, and that would be a pretty accurate position. The main flaw in that particular theory is that metric and decimal places were unheard of in the days of Nostradamus, and so would not be written in that manner. "Fire approaches the new City" is more likely to be a description of Villeneuve-sur-Lot in France. Villeneuve translated means new city, and it is positioned at 45 degrees latitude.

Example 2 has similarities to *Example 1*, but contains the extra twist of "Two steel birds will fall from the sky on the Metropolis", and of course "Within months,
Rivers will flow with blood. The undead will roam Earth for little time." What more can I say, this is just b****cks with a capital B. As for the un-dead roaming the earth, I think that the hoaxer should either cut down on their caffeine intake, or stop watching those old Hammer Horror movies!

For someone who died in 1566, I find it immensely clever that Nostradamus managed to write the quatrain illustrated in *Example 3* in the year 1654! With these facts it doesn't exactly take years of research to debunk this legend, but what is unusual is that the origins can be clearly traced. The fabricated quatrain was originally created in 1997 by Neil Marshal, a student of Brock University in Canada, and was printed as part of a web page essay. The idea was to point out how a fabricated prophecy can be created by using deliberate vague terms, and interoperated to predict most of the world's cataclysmic events. Ironic, me thinks!

Final Thoughts

This UL is a classic example of how people cling onto false presumptions, no matter how ludicrous, to try and make sense of a surreal situation. It is common that after any catastrophe people take reassurance in whichever way they can, and believing that it has already been mapped out in God's great plan helps make sense of the situation.

Nostradamus is one of the greatest historic figures and his name is known throughout the world, but whether his predictions are creditable are debatable. He has thousands of supporters the world over, but many believe that his quatrains are too vague and general, and that they can be associated with most of the great events throughout history. I have no doubt that this debate will continue to the end of time, which apparently Nostradamus has already predicted.

PROJECT 2067

NAME: The Starbucks Outrage
CODE: WT9804
ORIGIN: 11th September, 2001
STATUS: True

The Starbucks Outrage

On the fateful morning of September 11th 2001, rescue workers for the Brooklyn based Midwood Ambulance Service who were helping victims of the terrorist attack at "Ground Zero", asked at a local Starbucks Café for water for the victims. The rescue workers received three crates of bottled water, followed by a bill for $130! The shocked rescue workers had to dig in deep and settle the bill out of their own pockets.

Summary

So far, we have experienced many UL's that target big corporations with false accusations (e.g. Kentucky Fried Rat FD3301), but this shocking tale is disturbingly 100% true!

Not only did Starbucks charge $130 for three crates of water for what was needed to treat the victims of the attacks, the company completely ignored all calls and E-Mails from Ambulance officials concerned that their rescue workers had been overcharged. One caller who phoned the "Contact Us" telephone number on Starbucks website was rudely told that it simply could not have happened, and was thanked for his call!

Starbucks did eventually apologise for the outrage in the form of a personal call by the company's president Orin Smith, and a handwritten cheque to the Midwood Ambulance Service president Al Rapisarda for the amount of $130. The apology was sincere, but was only made after the whole affair was made public and had received a great deal of media coverage (mainly thanks to the persistent reporting of a Seattle journalist). The damage had already been done.

The greed of one manager at the Battery Park Plaza Starbucks should not cloud the fact that Starbucks donated free coffee and gifts to victims and rescue workers in the following days after the attack. Starbucks also officially closed for a day in respect for the victims of the terrorist atrocity, and donated $1 million to the September 11th Fund.

Final Thoughts

Obviously not reading the manual of 'how to make friends and influence people', Starbucks unbelievably made another public relations gaffe following the events of September the 11th. The storm was caused by advertising posters that had been erected on the walls of all the Starbucks outlets in the USA and Canada. The offending poster was for their brand of Tazo Citrus drinks, and showed two of the drinks standing side by side on grass in an extremely large and un-proportional sense (which could be seen as representing the twin towers), with a dragonfly flying towards the drinks. The slogan of the poster was "Collapse into cool", and it is that word "collapse" that probably linked all the visual images to the collapse of the twin towers in the public minds. During a sensitive time, this campaign was appallingly insensitive. Starbucks claimed that the advert was part of a long running campaign, but other companies aborted their campaigns with respect to the sensitivity of the moment, and movies that contained topical material even had their release dates delayed.

By using the code you can view the poster in question by visiting the Project 2067 website at:

www.project2067.com

PROJECT 2067

NAME: The $20 Dollar Prediction
CODE: WT9805
ORIGIN: 4th May 2002
STATUS: True

The $20 Prediction

```
INCREDIBLE THINGS HAPPEN IN AMERICA…
1°) Fold a $20 bill in half…
2°) Fold again, taking care to fold it exactly as
the picture shows (as seen at www.Project2067.com)
3°)  Fold the other end, exactly as before
     Et voilà, the PENTAGON on fire!!
4°)  Now, simply turn it over…
     The Twin Towers ablaze….


What a coincidience!  A simple geometric fold creates a
catastrophic premonition printed on all $20 bills!!!
```

Summary

This is a copy of a clever E-Mail that I received on 21/08/2002, almost a year after the terrorist attacks on America. If you look carefully on the notes, you may be able to see the web address http://www.testinadivitello.it/. I have checked out the website but it is in Italian and unfortunately I do not speak the lingo! But with little research I have discovered that the original version originates from the website www.allbrevard.net.

The website claims that one of their 'web guys' discovered this amazing coincidence while at a NASCAR party on 4th May 2002. A web page was created on the 9th May with the idea of sharing this find with friends. It was thought that only a dozen people would ever see the page but this proved to be an understated overview, 10 days later the hit counter had gone over the million mark, and now the web page has been viewed over 2 million times.

The original web page called this a coincidence, and that is all it is. This coincidental evidence of images portraying the 9/11 attacks was found by folding a $20 bill into different segments, but the art of folding notes and labels to find amusing pictures and messages has been a popular pastime for many years.

Final Thoughts

The US Treasury redesigned the present day $20 Dollar bill in 1998, and the folding of older notes will not achieve the same results.

By using the code you can view the pictures of the note being folded into the various positions on the Project 2067 website:

www.project2067.com

PROJECT 2067

NAME: It's A Lottery
CODE: WT9806
ORIGIN: New Jersey USA, 12/10/2001
STATUS: True

It's A Lottery

On the 12th November 2001, the talk of New Jersey was the bizarre coincidence of their 2 'Pick 3' lottery draws of that day. The morning numbers that were drawn were 5-7-8, and the draw later that day produced the numbers 5-8-7. These numbers make up the flight number of the American Airlines flight that crashed into the Queens area shortly after take-off on the same day that the numbers were drawn.

Summary

This amazing coincidence actually happened, the American Airlines flight number was 587. This news will not come as a shock to the hardened lottery player, as many pick numbers that are associated with events, signs or news events of that time. In fact, so many people picked the correct numbers on that day; the prize draw payout was only $16 per person, a lot lower than the average payout amount that is about $275.

Unusually, the New Jersey lottery only held one draw per day, and the day of the crash was the first time that two draws were held in the same day.

In another bizarre twist of fate, the lottery numbers drawn in a New York state lottery on 11th September 2001, exactly a year after the terrorist attacks, were 9-1-1. Enough said.

Final Thoughts

The plane crash on 12th November 2001 was not an act of terrorism and is not connected to the events of 9/11, but I feel that it is important enough to include under this section because of the direct effect it caused on the people of New York City, so soon after the terrorist atrocities on the World Trade Centre. The aircraft crashed in the New York area of Queens, which is a neighbourhood that many of the families of the firemen that lost their lives on 11th September lived.

236

9/11

This crash must have opened emotional wounds that were barely starting to heal, and I can imagine this new tragedy would have been too much to bear for the friends and family involved.

PROJECT 2067

```
NAME:      Pentagon Attack
CODE:      WT9807
ORIGIN:    Thierry Meyssan    (The Frightening Fraud)
STATUS:    False
```

Pentagon Attack

On 11th September 2001, shortly after the two planes collided with the towers of the World Trade Centre, reports were filtering in that there had been a large explosion at the Pentagon in Washington. At first it was reported that a large booby-trapped truck packed with explosives caused the explosion, but this was later denied and we were told that a plane crashing into one side of the Pentagon caused the damage.

It seems that there is more to this than meets the eye, and more than a hint of a conspiracy theory. In fact, some question the existence of American Airlines Flight 77, and whether a plane did crash into the Pentagon.

The following probing questions suggests that there could be an alternative explanation other than the official version of accounts:

1. Why is it that a Boeing 757 –200, weighing almost 100 tonnes and travelling at a speed of at least 250mph, only caused damage to the outer ring wall of the Pentagon?

2. How is it that a Boeing 757 that is 14.9 yards high, 51.7 yards long, with a wingspan of 41.6 yards and a cockpit 3.8 yards high, could crash into just the ground floor of this building?

3. How come no debris of the aircraft can be seen in the official photos of the aftermath of the incident?

4. Can you explain why the Defence Secretary deemed it necessary to sand over the lawn, which was otherwise undamaged after the attack?

5. What happened to the wings of the aircraft and why didn't they cause any damage to the building?

6. Why couldn't the County Fire Chief explain to reporters where the aircraft was?

238

7. Why is it that the aircraft's point of impact cannot be clearly identified in the official photos of the crash scene?

Did American Flight No.77 crash into the Pentagon, and if not, why is the American Government lying to everyone?

Summary

The French author Thierry Meyssan in his controversial book, The Frightening Fraud, first initiated this ambitious conspiracy theory. Thierry believes that the American Government is covering something up, and that a plane did not cause the damage to the Pentagon. Many believe that he is blowing hot air as he asks many probing questions, but cannot supply any explanations as answers. Right or wrong, a conspiracy theory was born.

Hot on the trail, a website was created. The 'Hunt The Boeing!' website mirrors the claim of Thierry Meyssan that an aircraft did not crash into the Pentagon, and asks the above questions to query the official account of what actually happened. Like many conspiracies, the supporting 'evidence' is selective and therefore inconclusive. There now seems as many websites debunking the theory as those that are promoting it, and the following are answers to the above questions.

Question 1: Why is it that a Boeing 757 –200, weighing almost 100 tonnes and travelling at a speed of at least 250mph, only caused damage to the outer ring wall of the Pentagon?

The satellite photos that this question is referring to is misleading because the photo only shows a Birdseye view of the intact roofs. What the photo does not show is that the crashed plane penetrated the outer ring, second ring and the third inner ring.

Also the question refers to the size, weight and speed of the aircraft, but does not take into consideration the size and robustness of the Pentagon. The plane may weigh almost 100 tonnes but it is mainly constructed out of a thin alloy material. Then take into consideration that the side of the Pentagon that the aircraft crashed into had recently been reinforced, and the walls were constructed using a combination of Potomac sand mixed in with steel reinforced concrete, with 10,000 concrete piles anchoring each side of the building, and an insertion of steel tubes designed to stop the building collapsing.

PROJECT 2067

Another point to make is that the aircraft hit the ground first before it hit the Pentagon, this initial impact would have absorbed most of the energy of the crash. The aircraft then hit the side of a solid reinforced building that has three times the floor space as the Empire State Building and is designed to shock absorb, it is not hard to see what will come out the worse.

On impact, the aircraft was travelling at a fraction of the speed as those that hit the World Trade Centre, which is mainly constructed using aluminium and glass. If you remember rightly, there wasn't a lot of the aircrafts remaining once they had passed through the building.

Taking all this into consideration, it is quite surprising that the aircraft that crashed into the Pentagon caused as much damage as it did!

Question 2: How is it that a Boeing 757 that is 14.9 yards high, 51.7 yards long, with a wingspan of 41.6 yards and a cockpit 3.8 yards high, could crash into just the ground floor of this building?

Again, the photograph that this question relates to is completely misleading. When looking at the photo the eyes naturally focus on where the fire engine is directing the hosed water onto the Pentagon, but the point of impact is actually more central to the photo and clearly shows two floors damaged. Another major point is that the aircraft hit the ground before ploughing into the Pentagon. As already explained in the answer to question one, hitting the ground first would have absorbed most of the energy of the crash.

The aircraft penetrated three of the five rings of the building.

Question 3: How come no debris of the aircraft is seen in the official photos of the aftermath of the incident?

The aircraft, full of jet fuel, crashed into the Pentagon and exploded into an intense fireball and disintegrated as it disappeared into the interior walls of the building (similar to what happened with the World Trade Centre Towers). Most of the aircraft would have been burned up completely, although the photo in reference to this question clearly shows debris.

Question 4: Can you explain why the Defence Secretary deemed it necessary to sand over the lawn, which was otherwise undamaged after the attack?

9/11

As it happens there is a quite simple explanation. In order to use heavy vehicles to clear away the debris, a temporary road was built across the soft lawn using sand and gravel.

Question 5: What happened to the wings of the aircraft and why didn't they cause any damage to the building?

The aircraft crashed into the ground at 45 degrees, and the wings would have disintegrated on impact with the explosion. What was left of the wings would have burned up as they were forced into the interior of the building. Besides, the wings quite clearly damaged the exterior of the building.

Question 6: Why couldn't the County Fire Chief explain to reporters where the aircraft was?

When a journalist asked Ed Plaugher, the Arlington County Fire Chief, "Is there anything left of the aircraft at all?"

Ed Plaugher replied, "First of all, the question about the aircraft, there are some small pieces of aircraft visible from the interior during this fire-fighting operation I'm talking about, but not large sections. In other words, there's no fuselage sections and that sort of thing."

"You know, I'd rather not comment on that. We have a lot of eyewitnesses that can give you better information about what actually happened with the aircraft as it approached. So we don't know. I don't know."

He was then asked, "Where is the jet fuel?"

The County Fire Chief replied, ""We have what we believe is a puddle right there that the -- what we believe is to be the nose of the aircraft. So -"

The vagueness of this quotation can be interpreted that the County Fire Chief is trying to cover something up, but the truth is probably that he was reluctant to make any assumptions about the situation before any hard evidence has been given. The Fire Chief was not stating that the puddle on the ground was aircraft fuel, he was in fact diverting from the stupid question that he was asked, and was simply stating that the puddle was probably melted metal from the nose of the aircraft.

Another small matter that needs to be mentioned is that the Fire Chief was asked, "Is there anything left of the aircraft at all?" from the journalist, and *not*, as the query claims, where the aircraft was? This slight diversion from the truth makes all the difference, and the question that was really asked was actually answered.

Question 7: Why is it that the aircraft's point of impact cannot be clearly identified in the official photos of the crash scene?

In most of the photos the point of impact is slightly obscured by smoke and water from the firemen's hoses, but like I said, it is only partially obscured and the point of impact can still be obviously identified in the photos.

Final Thoughts

Right or wrong, the debate will continue for many years to come, but I would like to ask a few more questions for you to ponder on, Why would the American Government want to go to such elaborate lengths to deceive the world that an aircraft crashed into the Pentagon? If an aircraft did not cause the damage, then what did cause it, and why lie about it? So, so many questions.

By using the code you can view all the pictures in question on the Project 2067 website:

www.project2067.com

9/11

```
NAME:      The Birmingham Warning
CODE:      WT9808
ORIGIN:    Unknown
STATUS:    False
```

The Birmingham Warning

This is not a joke or a hoax, this actually happened:

The other day I went around my mate's house straight from work. His wife answered the door and her first words were not "Hello" or "Hi, how are you?" They were "Don't go into Birmingham on the 6th October. At first I thought she was joking, but I soon realised that she was deadly serious.

When we had all sat down, she started to explain how her friend was shopping in the Cash and Carry when a man of Arabic appearance standing in front of her in the check-out queue did not have enough cash to pay for his goods. Noticing that the man was only a few quid short, she offered to make up the difference. The Arab man seemed very grateful, and when they went out into the car park, he spoke to her, "I would like to thank you for your kindness so I will give you this piece of advice, do not go into Birmingham Centre on 6th October".

Concerned of what she had just heard, the woman immediately contacted the police. They asked her to come down to the station and she was shown mug shots of local known Islamic terrorism supporters. It was not long before she spotted the man that she had spoken to.

As I have already said, this is a true story and the police are taking it as a serious threat. It all may account for nothing, but it is better to be safe than sorry.

```
Summary
```

This particular warning was rife at the end of September 2001, and was spreading via E-Mail and word of mouth. This legend was immediately condemned as a hoax, and the West Midlands Police Chief Constable, Edward Crew, stated that there is no intelligence to suggest there is any specific threat to the West Midlands. What is strange is that there was a terrorist bomb explosion in the Birmingham centre on 4th November 2001, but the attack was not carried

PROJECT 2067

out by an Islamic terrorist group, but by the 'Real IRA' instead. Although eerie, this must have been a coincidence as there are many variations to the legend, and the origins of the 'warning by a stranger' legends go back years.

Another similar version was circulating in London at the same time as the Birmingham warning. E-Mails were rapidly being sent round the offices telling a similar story, this time the shop in question was Harrods (a little bit more upmarket!), and the warning was not to travel on the tube. This really was playing on people's fears, as a gas attack on the tube is seen as a real and daunting potential threat.

In another variation a stranger warns of not going to Milton Keynes. In a city where everything has been created in block form, where the roads have more roundabouts than you could possibly imagine, and where the cows are even made up out of concrete, I cannot imagine why anyone would want to go there anyway. Perhaps the hoax warnings are a conspiracy from disgruntled Wimbledon FC supporters against their team's move to Milton Keynes!

Coventry is another city that was targeted by this latest bout of E-Mails, but there are many other places across the UK that have been used. In true UL fashion the variations are often localised to make a bigger impact and so are designed to cause maximum panic. There is no rational reason to believe the stories as there is no evidence to back it up, but because of the real threat of Islamic terrorism sweeping the world, the stories are seized upon and spread rapidly. This UL is playing with our present day anxieties and fears-that's what UL's do!

Before the Islamic terrorists were the perpetrators, the same legends were told about warnings of IRA bombings on the mainland. In these legends the man giving the warning often spoke with a soft Irish accent.

'Warning from a stranger' legends go a lot further back than that though, and the latest offerings may have evolved from legends like the one that was circulating around the US just after the bombing of Pearl Harbour in WW2. The story tells of a man giving a woman a lift in his car, and then the man refuses money that the lady has offered him for the petrol he has used. For this act of kindness, the woman offered to tell his fortune. She then predicted "There will be a dead body in your car before you get home, and Hitler will be dead in six months." The man then supposedly came across a car crash on his way home and attempted to take a seriously injured man to the local hospital, but the man died of his injuries en-route.

244

By the way, the other prediction about Hitler being dead in six months never materialised!

Final Thoughts

Check out the '*Liverpool Warning*', an amusing parody that arrived in my E-Mail Inbox late 2002, and investigated under the code **PD7302**

PROJECT 2067

NAME: Jackie Chan's Lucky Escape
CODE: WT9809
ORIGIN: September, 2001
STATUS: Undecided

Jackie Chan's Lucky Escape

All actors normally curse late scripts, but this particular one proved a blessing in disguise. Jackie Chan was supposed to act out a scene for the filming of an action comedy movie called Nosebleed. The screenwriters delivered the script late, and Jackie being the perfectionist that he is, decided to cancel that day's filming. Just as well really, as the scene was scheduled to be filmed at 7.00am on the morning of 11th September 2001 on top of one of the World Trade Centre's twin towers!

A shocked Jackie Chan quoted, "I would probably have died if the shooting had gone ahead as planned." Then adding in his typically straight but witty mannerism, "Well, I guess my time is not up yet!"

Because of the delayed script for the film Nosebleed, Jackie altered his plans at the 11th hour and started filming in Toronto for the film Tuxedo.

Summary

News that Jackie Chan was to star in an upcoming film called Nosebleed was filtering through movie buff channels back in 1999. Earlier articles reported that the plot of the film was that Jackie Chan was to star as a window cleaner at the World Trade Centre and accidentally overhears a terrorist plot to blow up the Statue of Liberty. Later, the plot was reported to be that Jackie Chan plays a window cleaner at the World Trade Centre, who takes a fancy to a waitress who works at the Windows Of The World Restaurant, which is situated at the top of the centre. Subsequently, the two get mixed up in a plot to blow up the World Trade Centre.

Whichever one of the versions you choose to believe, the plot of Nosebleed is certainly ironically eerie, but whether the shooting of the scene on top of the World Trade Centre was scheduled and then cancelled for the morning of 11th September is debatable.

The story of Jackie's lucky escape was first picked up by Asian news sources and was reported in newspapers such as the Singapore Strait Times, and was taken seriously enough to be documented in certain New York news sources as well. But one flaw of the legend has to be that Tuxedo is reported to have been scheduled to start filming on 10th September 2001, one day before the supposed scheduled filming of Nosebleed on top of the World Trade Centre. If the film Tuxedo was scheduled to start filming on that day in Toronto, it is highly unlikely that the filming of a scene in New York for another movie was scheduled for the next morning. The film industry simply doesn't work in that way!

Final Thoughts

Lucky escape and strange coincidence stories can be heard on most movie sets, and movie UL's deserve to have their own category. This category would include such legends like the ones that surrounded the suspicious death of Brandon Lee while filming *The Crow*, and the mysterious ghost like figure behind the net curtains in *3 Men And A Baby* (it turns out to be a cardboard cut out of Ted Danson that was accidentally left on the set during the shooting of that scene). I would love to explore the Movie Legends category another time.

PROJECT 2067

NAME: Coke Warning
CODE: WT9810
ORIGIN: 2002
STATUS: False

Coke Warning

A friend of my mother's was doing her weekly shopping at the local supermarket, when an Arab looking person in front of her didn't have enough money to pay for his shopping. Noticing that the difference in amount was only about 50p, my mother's friend offered to settle the difference, which the Arab looking bloke gratefully accepted.

When she was loading her shopping into the boot of her car, the Arab approached her and thanked her for helping him out and spoke these words of advice, "Please, I must warn you, do not drink any Coca Cola after the 1st June". With this he quickly left.

Summary

Sounds familiar? It should do! This is basically another variation of the 'warning from a stranger' legends, similar to the ones discussed in '*The Birmingham Warning*' (WT9808). The difference being that in this particular one the warning is about a product and not a place.

The product in question is Coca Cola, which makes this legend an interesting fusion between the typical 'warning from a stranger' legends and the old favourite 'Cokelore' legends. Coca Cola is an old campaigner in the weird and wonderful world of UL's, and the company's status as one of the world's most recognised products in the world has made it an easy target. Coca Cola could be seen as a symbolic product of the western world, and therefore a very believable target for Islamic terrorists hell bent on causing a spectacular catastrophe that would match the events of 9/11. Cokelore is discussed in greater detail in the 'Food & Drink' category. Check out the UL's *Cokecaine* (FD3306) and *Santa Coke* (FD3307).

Final Thoughts

The Coca Cola website (Coca-Cola.com, *not* Coca-Cola.co.uk) states, 'These rumours are absolutely false and are causing needless worry.' The American based website also debunks many other false rumours of Cokelore and is truly worth a visit.

PROJECT 2067

NAME: The Devil's Face In Smoke
CODE: WT9811
ORIGIN: September 11th, 2001
STATUS: Undecided

The Devil's Face In Smoke

Freelance photographer Mark D Phillips took photos of the World Trade Centre just after the second aircraft had hit it from the top of his apartment building in Brooklyn. One of the photos appears to show a demonic face shaped out of the rising smoke from one of the towers.

Summary

Folk used to claim that a camera never lies, but in this age of digital technology we know differently. Images can be doctored, distorted, manipulated and airbrushed with such ease it can basically be achieved by any 10 year old with a computer. Different photos of images of the *devil face* in the smoke have immerged since the terrorist attacks of 9/11, all thought to be fake. But the black and white photograph taken by Mark D Phillips is supposed to be 100% genuine.

Mr. Phillips is a respected photographer who has worked with the Associated Press for 15 years. The photo was one of many that were sold to the Associated Press and were transmitted within 40 minutes after the event. Mark D Phillips is thought to have complied with the strict guidelines by the AP that prohibits the alteration of photos in any way.

O.K. We now know that the photo is probably genuine, but what are we actually looking at? As always, it can be interpreted in many different ways. One theory is that it proves that Satan's power was resident in the World Trade Centre. The image is proof that Satan had been awakened and was fleeing his place of residence. The theory then claims that the World Trade Centre was the root of all evil causing 2nd and 3rd world debt, and the terrorists are actually martyrs ridding the world of evil.

The most popular belief is that the image of Satan appeared out of bellowing smoke as a sign of the great act of evil that had taken place and as a warning of the evil that is at large in our world.

Of course, some may say that it is simply a coincidence, similar to seeing faces in the clouds. Whatever you believe, the photo taken by Mr. Philips has certainly generated a few lively debates!

Final Thoughts

You may have seen a another colour photograph of the '*devil's face in the smoke*'. This photo was widely used by news corporations such as CNN, but Mark D Philips did not take that photo and so cannot verify its authenticity.

By using the code you can view the picture of the *devil's face in the smoke* on the Project 2067 website:

www.project2067.com

PARODIES...

INTRODUCTION..PAGE 254

BIN LADEN'S MEMO..PAGE 256

THE LIVERPOOL WARNING...................................PAGE 258

BODY PARTS...PAGE 260

ULs OF ULs..PAGE 262

PROJECT 2067

Thursday 18th, August
16.15: The Office

CATEGORY: PARODIES

What does the word parody mean? In UL terms a parody is an imitation legend used for comical effect. A parody legend may contain segments from all different kinds of UL's and cleverly moulded together into an amusing tale. For a good example I must warn you about a new computer virus that may find it's way into your inbox called the 'Gullibility Virus'. As soon as it is opened it makes people believe and forward copies of ridiculous hoax E-Mails relating to anything from cookie recipes, internet taxes, computer viruses, sick kids trying to beat some kind of world record, nostradamus predictions, to warnings from strangers in exchange for a kind deed. Once infected, the immune system to hoaxes and tall stories completely breaks down, and you end up believing anything you read on the Internet. This is not a hoax, and you can tell how serious this is by the amount of exclamation marks I am using!!!!!!!! Please pass this message onto everyone you know. For every message forwarded, the 'hopelessly gullible charity' will donate one pound to itself!

As you may have guessed, the above warning is told with the tongue firmly placed in the cheek, but does hit a chord of truth with the suggestion that people will believe anything they read on the Internet. This is a good example of how parody legends use sarcasm and satire to comical effect. In other words, a parody legend is basically taking the Mick.

I hope you will find the following small collection of parodies amusing. *Bin Ladens Memo* (PD7301) is hilarious and comes as light relief from the hundreds of legends that have emerged from the events of 9/11. The *Liverpool Warning* (PD3302) follows with a similar vein, but is written with a serious tone and has a slight twist. The other parody legend I would like to mention is *UL Of UL's* (PD7304). This is unique, as it is an accusation of a Government conspiracy aimed at the UL websites that investigate and debunk legends. Confused? You will be!

This is it; I am wrapping the project up. I am flying back to London tomorrow morning and will present my findings to Max who will meet me at Heathrow. I think that Max will be pleasantly surprised, as my digging into the murky depths of the UL world has uncovered some interesting pointers. I will explain all this in greater detail in due time. Meanwhile, I will have to clear out my 'shoebox' and pack up all my belongings. In a weird way I will miss the 'shoebox' (apart

PARODIES

from the smell), as this cramped working space as become my haven from the mad and crazy world that exists outside of the window. Also, it has helped me to appreciate certain things in life, like the fact that I have never suffered from claustrophobia!

I have gathered all my notes and findings, and shall write up my project conclusion on the plane tomorrow. It will help kill a few hours and provide light relief from the in-flight entertainment system (no doubt there will be an episode of the Simpsons that I have seen at least 20 times before, and if I am lucky, an episode of Mr.Bean, to which I would have seen too many times to keep count). Tomorrow is another day and I am going to forget about work and go out for a few drinks tonight. I am not sure which bar to go to, but I will certainly take a wide berth around Charlie's. Don't worry, I won't get plastered, I will have enough to worry about tomorrow without having the extra hassle of having a throat as rough as a pair of builders testicles and my head feeling like it will explode from the inside.

PROJECT 2067

NAME: Bin Laden's Memo
CODE: PD7301
ORIGIN: 12 October, 2001
STATUS: False

Bin Laden's Memo

From: Bin Laden, Osama [mailto:osama@taliban.com]

Sent: Saturday, November 17, 2001 10.15AM

To: Cave mates

Subject: The Cave

Hi guys. We've all been putting in long hours but we've really come together as a group and I love that. Big thanks to Omar for putting up the poster that says, "There is no 'I' in team" as well as the one that says "Hang In There, Baby." That cat is hilarious. However, while we are fighting a jihad, we can't forget to take care of the cave. And frankly I have a few concerns.

First of all, while it's good to be concerned about cruise missiles, we should be even more concerned about the scorpions in our cave. Hey, you don't want to be stung and neither do I, so we need to sweep the cave daily. I've posted a sign-up sheet near the main cave opening.

Second, it's not often I make a video address but when I do, I'm trying to scare the most powerful country on earth, okay? That means that while we're taping; please do not ride your razor scooter in the background. Just while we're taping. Thanks.

Third point, and this is a touchy one. As you know, by edict, we're not supposed to shave our beards. But I need everyone to just think hygiene, especially after mealtime. We're all in this together.

Fourth: food. I bought a box of Wotsits recently, clearly wrote "Osama" on the front, and put it on the top shelf. Today, my Wotsits were gone. Consideration. That's all I'm saying.

Finally, we've heard that there may be American soldiers in disguise trying to infiltrate our ranks. I want to set up patrols to look for them. First patrol will be Omar, Muhammad, Abdul, Akbar, and Bob.

Love you lots.

Osama

PARODIES

Summary

First aired on an American National Public Radio show called "Rewind" on the 12th October 2001, it soon spread globally in the form of E-Mails. John Moe was the original author of this memo, and wrote it for "Rewind" which is a satire news programme. It has been repeated on many other radio shows since, including the old Chris Tarrant Morning Show for Capital FM 95.8 (London).

With the depressing shadow of global terrorism cast boldly over our heads, it is refreshing to see a satire sideswipe at the whole situation. The thought of the most wanted man in the world running his camp of ruthless terrorists like a girl guide group brings a smile to my face. As for the phrase "There is no 'I' in team", it is more like a business 'buzz phrase' used by a second rate manager in the faceless concrete office blocks of Slough, than by a dangerous Islamic militant holed up in the caves of Afghanistan.

Bin Laden's Memo is a parody of all the UL's, hoaxes, and rumours associated with 9/11 and the all the hysteria that surrounds them. By turning the worlds most wanted man into some sort of comical caricature, it helps to bring perspective to the situation and to suppress our fears.

Final Thoughts

During World War Two, cartoons and songs about Adolf Hitler were used as propaganda by the allies. Hitler was portrayed as a silly little man with a ridiculous moustache, and one famous song even declared that 'Hitler has only got one ball, the other is in the Albert Hall'. It was this kind of humour that lifted the morale of the British people during the Blitz and helped keep alive the famous British spirit.

PROJECT 2067

NAME: Liverpool Warning
CODE: PD7302
ORIGIN: Unknown
STATUS: False

Liverpool Warning

> Normally I don't fall for this kind of thing, but a few
> people here have mentioned it and I think there could be
> something in it...
>
> Beware!
>
> I got this today and the warning is genuine!
>
> Yesterday, a friend was travelling on a Paris to London
> flight. A man of Arabic appearance got off the plane and
> my friend noticed that he had left his bag behind. She
> grabbed the bag and ran after him, caught up with him in
> the terminal and handed him back his bag. He was extremely
> grateful and reached into his bag, which appeared to
> contain large bundles of money.
>
> He looked around to make sure nobody was looking and
> whispered "I can never repay your kindness, but I will try
> to.... with a word of advice for you: Stay away from
> Liverpool".
>
> My friend was genuinely terrified. "Is there going to be
> an attack?" she asked him.
>
> "No ... ", he whispered back...... "It's a sh*thole."

Summary

This is a copy of an E-Mail sent to me on 14/11/02, and is a parody of the
Birmingham Warning (WT9808). I thought this version was true to form of the
UL until the very end, when the punch line caught me hook, line, and sinker!

The Liverpool Warning came onto the scene just before the Christmas period,
on the back of government warnings of possible terrorist attacks and advice to be

PARODIES

vigilant at all times. It was a time of great anxiety and came amongst a growing fear that the enemy is within.

This was a light-hearted poke in the eye to all the hoaxes and legends that were cluttering up our in-trays, and provides humour to a very serious and sensitive climate. It is a sarcastic dig at how vulnerable and gullible we all are.

Final Thoughts

Liverpool isn't that bad…Honest!

PROJECT 2067

```
NAME:      Body Parts
CODE:      PD7303
ORIGIN:    Unknown
STATUS:    False
```

Body Parts

Most of you have read the scare-mail about the person whose kidneys were stolen while he was passed out. While that was an "urban legend," this one is NOT. It's happening every day. I'm sending this "warning" only to a few of my closest friends. You too may have been a victim ... read on.

My thighs were stolen from me during the night of August 3rd a few years ago. It was just that quick. I went to sleep in my body and woke up with someone else's thighs. The new ones had the texture of cooked oatmeal. Who would have done such a cruel thing to legs that had been wholly, if imperfectly, mine for years? Whose thighs were these? What happened to mine?

I spent the entire summer looking for them. I searched, in vain, at pools and beaches, anywhere I might find female limbs exposed. I became obsessed. I had nightmares filled with cellulite and flesh that turns to bumps in the night. Finally, hurt and angry, I resigned myself to living out my life in jeans and Sheer Energy pantyhose.

Then, just when my guard was down, the thieves struck again. My rear end was next. I knew it was the same gang, because they took pains to match my new rear end (although badly attached at least three inches lower than the original) to the thighs they had stuck me with earlier. Now my rear complemented my legs, lump for lump. Frantic, I prayed that long skirts would stay in fashion.

Two years ago I realized my arms had been switched. One morning while fixing my hair, I watched, horrified but fascinated, as the flesh of my upper arms swung to and fro with the motion of the hairbrush. This was really getting scary. My body was being replaced, cleverly and fiendishly, one section at a time. In the end, in deepening despair, I gave up my T-shirts.

What could they do to me next? Age? Age had nothing to do with it. Age was supposed to creep up, unnoticed and intangible, something like maturity. NO, I was being attacked, repeatedly and without warning. That's why I've decided to share my story. I can't take on the medical profession by myself. Women of the

PARODIES

world, wake up and smell the coffee! That isn't really "plastic" those surgeons are using. You know where they're getting those replacement parts, don't you? The next time you suspect someone has had a face "lifted," look again! Was it lifted from you? Check out those tummy tucks and buttocks raisings. Look familiar? Are those your eyelids on that movie star? I think I finally may have found my thighs... and I hope that Cindy Crawford paid a really good price for them!

This is NOT a hoax! This is happening to women in every town every night. ....Warn your friends!!!!!!!

Summary

This story is a parody of 'The Kidney Heist' (CR1708) and was obviously written by a woman who doesn't believe in growing old gracefully. The strange thing is, this happens to all of us in the end!

A close friend forwarded this E-Mail on to me on 21/11/2001, and he has no recollection of who sent him the original E-Mail. The E-Mail was written in very large font and was illustrated with cartoon style characters.

Final Thoughts

I think that the same thing happened to my last girlfriend, thieves struck during the night and stole her perky peaches and replaced them with droopy melons.

PROJECT 2067

NAME: The UL of UL's
CODE: PD7304
ORIGIN: Unknown
STATUS: Undecided

The UL of UL's

One report claims that research has proved that Urban Legend books and websites are actually Urban Legends themselves. It is claimed that these sources claim stories are legends when they are actually true.

Why, you may ask, would anyone bother with such a deception? The reason is part of a global conspiracy to deceive the masses. After all, what better way is there to cover up incriminating and embarrassing situations than to spread them as rumours and have them debunked as Urban Legends. This propaganda directly targets the well educated and the politically influential people in society into deceptively believing in what they think is the 'truth'.

The registration address of many of the popular Urban Legend websites clearly shows a US Government address. This address, usually the CIA, clearly proves the US Government's involvement in these sites. One CIA official has said that the Government's involvement is "classified", and that the CIA is merely trying to "keep the American public properly informed by discrediting allegations that could jeopardize the ability of our leaders to govern effectively."

Do not believe everything you read.

Summary

A conspiracy theory about the very people that supply us with information about conspiracy theories, whatever next? This theory originated from a document called "The Dredged Report" and is dated 02/01/99, and can be found at the AFU & Urban Legends Website (www.urbanlegends.com). I have found out little information on "The Dredged Report" and at the time of print have not had a response from the AFU & Urban legends website to which I have E-Mailed an enquiry. Although, it seems to me that this report is actually a spoof of the Drudge Report. The Drudge Report features cutting edge news by the infamous columnist Matt Drudge whose website is viewed by millions on a daily basis.

I love the ironic tone of this parody as it has turned the tables on the most popular UL websites on the Internet. It also throws up an interesting theory and triggers many "what if?" questions. What if certain government agencies did control these websites? It is certainly possible, and this tactic could be used to debunk rumours that may be true but damaging to a country's interests. This would be an ingenious way to control the information that we are fed as it targets the very people that are sceptical of how much truth we are given and thrive on conspiracy theories.

Final Thoughts

Who can you believe? As Mulder and Scully once said 'The truth is out there!'

FINAL REPORT...

INTRODUCTION...PAGE 266

CONCLUSION...PAGE 267

THE SCIENCE BIT...PAGE 270

BUZZWORDS & JARGON...PAGE 272

RESEARCH - BOOKS...PAGE 273

RESEARCH - WEBSITES...PAGE 275

FINAL WORD..PAGE 277

PROJECT 2067

Final Report

I hate air travel. Well, no, that isn't exactly right, what I should say is that I hate travelling economy class! The thought of travelling 250mph while 30,000 feet above solid ground would be a little easier if I was sipping champagne and enjoying the choice of food from a menu that has been prepared by some fancy chef (who probably has a French name), while enjoying all the other luxury trappings of First Class. Instead, I have to settle for a miniature "mini me" can of coke or a glass of cat pee that passes as white wine, while enjoying the set menu of a rubbery substance they call chicken with soggy chips. This didn't deter Roger who took up seats E2 and E3 next to me. This man hulk has too many similarities to Jabba The Hut (from Return Of The Jedi. You remember, the one with Princess Leia looking fit in that weird gold bikini!), has obviously never heard of lettuce, and has so many chins he must have one for every occasion! Not only did I learn his name, I learnt that he is a double-glazing salesman from Texas, and likes apple pie and custard (I know this last fact because he must have eaten mine while I went to the toilet).

Deodorant! Deodorant is a word that Roger has obviously never heard of, not only does he look like a pig, he also smells like one as well. Roger is the type of bloke that breaks out into a mad sweat every time he moves a muscle. Even though the air-conditioning is on full, beads of sweat are pouring off his shiny big forehead and onto his sweat stained trousers. The damp patches under his blue cotton shirt are steadily increasing in size, if they get much bigger they could have filmed "Waterworld" under his arms. I have tried to take my mind off the smell by listening to the in-flight radio but I have two ripped wires instead of earpieces. This is going to be a *very* long flight. Just as well I suppose, as I have a huge amount of work to finish before we reach Heathrow.

I can't wait to get back home. I have missed talking about the weather, having cups of tea, watching match of the day on Saturday night, going down the local (a *real* pub, not those depressing bars in NY which double as a meeting place for lonely depressed men, usually on executive burnout) and having a pint of lager (decent lager, not the gnats piss they drink over there). On the other hand, I am returning to a country that is addicted to soups, DIY and reality TV. Still, there is no place like home!

Conclusion

So, do I have a story? The simple answer to that is yes. There is more to UL's than idle gossip told during those ritual 'office water cooler conversations' that take place at three o'clock most afternoons in most offices, and those who know this can realise the full potential of how they work. Used in the right way, this knowledge can be used as a very powerful psychological weapon, and the most obvious proof of this is when UL's are used as wartime propaganda. It is believed that both Hitler and Churchill used the UL channels as propaganda tools to their full effect during World War 2, as the two leaders played out tactical warfare like a game of chess trying to outwit each other. Great examples of this can be seen in *Carrot Vision* (FD3308) and *The Wooden Airfield* (TR8714), as both legends were used during World War 2 as smoke screens to disguise the real hidden agendas behind the decoys. Manipulation of this kind is an old tried and tested technique but is increasingly being use as a tactic in modern warfare. The American term for this tactic is 'psychops', this propaganda technique was well documented during the Iraqi conflict of 2003. The Iraqi Information Minister (remember, the one that had the Frank Spencer beret!) took the idea of propaganda to the extreme when he was telling the Iraqi people on live TV that the Iraqis were winning the war. This may have sounded convincing if it wasn't for the fact that whilst he was making this claim, US tanks were rolling through the streets of Baghdad behind him. There is no doubt though that when correctly applied, UL's of this kind can boost morale amongst allies, and at the same time can crush the belief of the enemy. They can blind the truth and cause confusion when needed. They say that news travels fast, but believe me, rumours travel faster. So what better way is there to spread confusion or to instigate unrest amongst enemy ranks than the spread of a well designed but concocted rumour?

There are other areas where the use of UL's can be exploited, and recently it has been used for commercial gains in the entertainment market. *The Blair Witch Project* (HO4608) was one of the top grossing films of 1999. Not bad for a film that was made on a shoestring budget. One of the main reasons for this is the hysteria that the Website had caused before the film was even released. In what only can be described as a huge publicity coup, the people behind the Blair Witch Project devised an innovative way to market their film. The website contained a colourful and detailed history of the Blair Witch legend (completely fabricated!), and explained that the film is the actual footage found in the cameras of the students that went missing while investigating the legend. People believed all this to be true and it became a major talking point causing great controversy, and in turn, great publicity. The film was waited upon with much anticipation and it was a huge hit when it was finally released. By setting up a simple website as the canvas of the manufactured legend, they allowed the process of UL's to do the business for them. This is a cheap, simple, but highly effective way to market a product. It just goes to prove that you do not need to spend millions of pounds on advertising campaigns to get a product noticed.

Not only can the power of UL's work positively for a product or company, it can also have the opposite effect with devastating consequences. In most situations it is unclear where these vicious rumours start from, they may be concocted by business rivals, or simply by someone with a grudge against that particular company. Large corporations such as Coca Cola, KFC, Disney and Microsoft seem to be relentlessly targeted in what only can be described as hate campaigns. Some may see this as a justified stand against these huge faceless corporations that have muscled smaller competitors out of their way to try and monopolise their particular markets; A typical David vs. Goliath scenario. People believe that certain corporations are not acting in the best interests of their customers because they are too consumed in their own greed and lust for money.

Another more seedy theory is that companies are spreading malicious rumours about their competitors to try and discredit them. This is often thought to be the case but is hardly ever proved through lack of evidence. Everyone knows that this sort of thing goes on in the cutthroat world of business, but it is still a dangerous game to play, as it would be a 'PR' disaster to get caught in the act. This sort of practice would be heavily frowned upon by the public and would be seen as dirty tricks.

Often, the origins of UL's are not so calculated and manufactured, but a reflection of the fears and anxieties of a particular period in time. A lot of the time the same UL will appear again and again, decade after decade, adjusting itself to fit in with the modern society. The best example of this is the *Vanishing Hitchhiker* (HR4704), which has been told in one form or another since the days of the Bible. Throughout the ages the motifs have remained virtually the same, but the legends adapts itself into the different time periods. The best example of this is the mode of transport that is used to pick up the hitchhiker, in modern versions it is a car, but they didn't have cars in the 18th century, so in those days it was a horse and cart, centuries before that it was a bare backed rider. This is what a true UL does, mutate and adapt to the wings of change or to the different needs of different cultures. This is how legends pass the test of time. Put it this way, do you think the *Vanishing Hitchhiker* would still have the same effect and be as popular as it is today if the mode of transport was still a horse and cart? I doubt it!

FINAL REPORT

Old campfire favourite like the *The Hook* (HR4702) and *Knock Knock Knock* (HR4703) reflects the changing attitudes and values of teenage girls in the 1950's, and how much of a threat it was seen to the very fabric of American society. Dormitory life at American colleges was greatly improved during the 50's, and a relaxation of many rules gave the students a new sense of freedom. With this newfound freedom and the arrival of Rock 'N' Roll, girls started asserting themselves in society in a way that was completely unheard of before. The parents of this new generation did not approve or understand these changes but felt helpless to withstand it. So the moral judgements of a society concocted these legends as warnings to girls to be careful, highlighting how harsh the punishment may be if they strayed off this straight and narrow moral path and drop their guard. Extreme? Yes, but they must have had some kind of impact because at almost every camp fire there has been since, these legends have been told, both frightening and enthralling the audience. These legends are bare-boned, pure and simple; the best form of horror.

The arrival of Netlore has permanently changed the face of ULs forever. Some academics believe that the Internet has killed off the UL as we knew it, as it is now more about popular culture and less about folklore. It is true that hearing a story from a friend is far more interesting than reading it on a monitor screen, as the computer lacks the interactive effect of facial expressions and gestures that help bring colour to a tale, not to mention the social aspect. On the other hand, the Internet has helped to accelerate the spread of ULs to the global scene at lightening speed. For anyone with an interest in ULs, the Internet has made research so much more accessible with superb websites such as Snopes.com, although websites can never be a substitute for books such as the ones written by Jan Harold Brunvand.

Just like a UL may change and adapt to present situations, the whole structure and medium of UL's must do the same. Maybe the resentment of Netlore is a fear of new technology, a topic covered with it's own UL category! I do not feel that the growth of Netlore is a threat to the traditional UL; it is a mere change in direction to keep up with the ever-shifting sands of time.

The Science Bit

As with most subjects under the sun, UL's can be mind-bogglingly dissected with a scientific approach to the investigation. No, I am not joking, *there* is a scientific approach. Think about it, if they can spend years studying the way Beckham bends the ball in the name of science, they can turn *anything* into a scientific subject. So, here is the science bit:

One scientific definition for UL's is that they are "mind viruses". This is a good definition as there are strong similarities. Just like a virus, UL's usually appear inexplicably and spontaneously spread from person to person with the amount of people it "infects" multiplying after each case. One theory is that each person may tell five other people the story that they have heard. The following table illustrates how this theory may work on that basis:

Time	Added	Cumulative
0	1	1
1	5	2
2	25	7
3	125	32
4	625	157
5	3,125	782
6	15,625	3,907
7	78,125	19,532
8	390,625	97,657
9	1,953,125	488,282
10	9,765,625	2,441,407

This table illustrates how vastly a legend can spread in such a short space of time, but there is one major flaw to this theory. A lot of people share the same group of friends, so therefore the same individual may hear the same legend from two or more of their friends. To counteract this problem, it is presumed that each friend shares on average 3.5 of another friend friends (still following me?). The following table shows the new results:

FINAL REPORT

Time	Added	Cumulative
0	1	1
1	2	2
2	2	4
3	3	6
4	5	9
5	8	14
6	11	22
7	17	33
8	26	50
9	38	76
10	58	114

This is all very well, but one of the beauties about UL's is the fact that a version may vary from telling to telling in the same concept as the game of Chinese Whispers. I may hear a version from you and pass this on to another friend. My friend's version is still probably very similar to your version, but if my friend then heard the story from someone else entirely (not in the same social network), then that version is likely to be varied from your version. Diagram 1.A on the website demonstrates this theory, but it can be taken as a golden rule that we can presume that the closer the versions are to the origin of the UL, the less likely they are to vary from each other. The versions will vary greater as they move further away from the origin. Mind you, you don't exactly have to be Einstein to work that one out (it still has probably taken a team of University students 3 years to come up with these results!).

Buzzwords & Jargon

Sometimes it may seem that people in the UL circle are speaking in code, and you feel like you are trying to infiltrate some kind of secret society. Like in any interest, hobby, sport or subject, the small world of UL's does have its own terminology. The following is a short list of Urban Legend jargon and buzzwords and their meanings:

Terms used for "Urban Legend":

UL
Urban Myths
Urban Folklore
FOAF
Modern Folklore
Kentucky Fried Rat tales
Contemporary Folklore
Dead Cat stories
Office water cooler conversations
Monkey Burgers

FOAF: "Friend Of A Friend". Term coined meaning Urban Legends, as usually they begin with 'This happened to a friend of a friend…'

Monkey Burgers: Urban Legends in the Netherlands are called "*Broodje aap verhalen*", which translates into English as "Monkey Burgers".

Proto-Legend: A potential legend at the beginning stage of the process, that may or may not turn into an Urban Legend.

Netlore: Urban Legends that are narrated with the use of E-Mail and the Internet.

Faxlore: Term used when an Urban Legend is narrated with the use of a Fax machine.

Motif: Common subject matter found in all versions of an Urban Legend and across different legends. For example, The Hook has the motifs "a maniac with a hook for a hand".

FINAL REPORT

Variant: Usually meaning a different version of a legend.

Parody: Imitation legend used for comical effect.

Research

Researching the origins of ULs is a long and painstaking business if not sometimes impossible, but there are certain books and websites out there that may make life a little easier. The people who have written these books and websites are often experts in the field and have dedicated their lives to the research of ULs. You probably would have noticed that I have mentioned Jan Harold Brunvand a few times throughout the project and I have listed a few of his books below. In truth, any one of his many books would be a worthy read as they are not only interesting, but also written in a very concise and clear manner. Jan H Brunvand was a professor at the University of Utah and is extremely well respected in UL circles, but unfortunately he will not be writing any more books as he is now retired. He has informed me that he is enjoying his retirement, spending his time fly fishing, skiing, and seeing his grandchildren. I wish him the very best in his retirement and would like to thank him for his help when it was requested.

One website in particular is worth a visit, and that is Snopes.com. This extremely well designed and informative website is written by David and Barbara Mikkelson, who seem to work tirelessly researching any legend under the sun.

Books:

```
Title:          The Vanishing Hitchhiker
Author:         Jan Harold Brunvand
Published By:   W.W.Norton & Company
```

Jan H Brunvand's first novel and a must for anyone with even the slightest interest in ULs. First published in 1981, this book gives a thorough and interesting insight into all the classics. The book is supposed to be about American Urban Legends and their meanings, but Brunvand has since stated that this was an over sight as many of the legends are told all over the world. This is raw and energetic, in other words, a classic. The book also contains an excellent chapter named "Collecting and Studying Urban Legends". A *must* for your collection.

Title: The Baby Train
Author: Jan Harold Brunvand
Published by: W.W.Norton & Company

The Baby Train is a no-nonsense collection of ULs and their meanings. Worth buying for the "A Type-Index Of Urban Legends" section.

Title: Too Good To Be True
Author: Jan Harold Brunvand
Published By: W.W.Norton & Company

A large and colourful collection of Urban Legends and their meanings, in a well thought out format.

Title: Urban Legends
Author: N.E. Genge
Published By: Three Rivers Press, New York

A large collection of Urban Legends delivered in a fast and frantic style. The book is an interesting read although individual legends cannot be easily located, and the style of writing can sometimes be disjointed and confusing.

Title: Alligators In The Sewer And 222 Other
                Urban Legends
Author: Thomas J. Craughwell
Published By: Black Dog & Leventhal Publishers

A head rush of 222 legends in this basic but fun collection. This "easy-read" book is written in a stylish and well- organised manner. It's only let down is the fact that no meanings or origins of the legends are offered.

FINAL REPORT

Websites:

Website Name: **Snopes**
Website Address: **www.snopes.com**

This well designed website is comprehensive and easy to navigate, but most importantly, it is simply the best source for information concerning UL's that you will find on the net. I don't think David and Barbara Mikkelson (the authors) know the meaning of the word "sleep", as they seem to work 24-7 researching and debunking any legend that comes on the scene, and I mean *any* legend. If you need to check the details of a particular legend, this site should be one of your first ports of call.

I personally think that Snopes came into their own with their coverage of legends following 9/11. The sheer volume of UL's and rumours was tremendous, but Snopes managed to provide an accurate analysis of the legends almost immediately after they had emerged. When everybody didn't know what to believe and what not to, Snopes excelled.

Website Name: **The AFU & Urban Legends Archive**
Website Address: **www.urbanlegends.com**

A large and comprehensive archive of Urban legends with a couple of cool features. The best probably being the Urban Legend Zeitgeist, where you can check out all the latest Urban Legends. Another being the Urban Legend Vortex, where you can study UL's from the different hemispheres.

Website Name: **Urban Legends.about**
Website Address: **www.urbanlegends.about.com**

Easy to navigate but not in the same ball park as Snopes. Still worth a visit

Website Name: **Monkey Burgers**
Website Address: **www.4urbanlegends.4anything.com**

The Monkey Burgers website by the colourful Patrick Arink as mentioned in *Cleaning Up With Toothpaste* (AW1909). This Dutch website is very basic but fun, and you may find a hidden gem!

Website Name: Official Darwin Awards/legends
Website Address: www.darwinawards.com

Part of the official Darwin Awards website, this section deals with apocryphal stories of bogus Darwinian efforts. If you still do not know what the Darwin Awards is all about, check out *The JATO Rocket Car* (TR8711) for a full description.

Website Name: Hunt The Boeing Website
Website Address: www.asile.org/citoyens/numero13/
                        pentagone/erreurs_en.htm

Well worth the numb fingers and cramp wrist from typing in the address. This website explains in great detail the conspiracy theory that is *Pentagon Attack* (WT9807), and illustrates this with photos from the crash scene.

Final Word

I am now bringing the project to a close. The plane has now started it's decent and the familiar green fields of England that are rolling beneath are now frequently being interrupted by rooftops and roads. I can now see the M25 winding its way through the countryside like an ugly snake as the plane takes one final turn for the approach into Heathrow. I have had time to reflect on the present situation and one question keeps resurfacing like a boil on the butt, is Project 2067 enough to save the paper? If I am being completely honest with myself then the answer is "no chance!" One point of interest may pull in a few more punters for a while, but it is only delaying the inevitable. Lets face it, what chance does the Daily National have against the media might of Agnus Brute. Brute is determined to build an empire that will monopolise the media industry and he sees the Daily National as one little bug to wipe of his windscreen en-route.

This is hardly a new revelation, I guess I had realised that the paper was doomed even before I took on the project. That's why I insisted on carrying out the project in New York, I have always wanted to visit the city and saw this as my chance. Of course I had to blag my reasons (I said something about mainly researching the origins of American urban mythology), but at the end of the day, not many questions were asked and so not many answers were provided. Probably not the most honest thing I have ever done in my life, but I was hardly going to kick a gift horse in the mouth, was I?

I hope you have enjoyed Project 2067 as much as I have, I think it has been a learning curve for all of us. We have only scratched the surface of ULs, but it has been enough to understand the mechanism and structure of ULs, how they are spread, and how they are effectively used for moral and propaganda purposes. You should also now be able to spot the traits of an UL when you read or are being told a story, and this will help in the prevention of spreading harmful rumours or bogus virus alerts. Just remember, if it happened to a friend of a friend, the story is probably as viable as Elvis driving a 57 bus through Tooting high street, and if the story is too good to be true, then it probably isn't!

The aircraft has stopped circling Heathrow and is now preparing to land. The "Please fasten your seatbelts" sign has now illuminated so I will have to be quick. I bet you have wondered why this assignment was called Project 2067, well the answer is simply...I don't believe it, I am now being instructed to turn off my laptop by the lovely stewardess who looks like she shares the same make-up artist as Marilyn Manson. I had better go, I will tell you another time.

QUICK GUIDE STATUS SUMMARY

CLASSIC HORROR...

BACKSEAT HITCHHIKER	HR4701	FALSE
THE HOOK	HR4702	UNDECIDED
KNOCK, KNOCK, KNOCK	HR4703	FALSE
THE VANISHING HITCHHIKER	HR4704	UNDECIDED
BLOODY MARY	HR4705	FALSE
THE ROOMMATE'S DEATH	HR4706	FALSE
LIGHTS OUT	HR4707	FALSE

JUST FOR LAUGHS...

FART IN THE DARK	CM1601	UNDECIDED
THE COLLEGE LETTER	CM1602	UNDECIDED
THE PARISIAN BELLBOY	CM1603	UNDECIDED
STAND OFF AT SEA	CM1604	FALSE
THE CAT FLAP	CM1605	FALSE
THE BISCUIT BULLET	CM1606	FALSE
THE BRICKLAYER	CM1607	UNDECIDED
THE NAKED SKIER	CM1608	UNDECIDED
TAKE THE TUBE	CM1609	FALSE
THE UNZIPPED FLY	CM1610	FALSE

CRIME...

THE STING	CR1701	UNDECIDED
THE BODY IN THE BED	CR1702	TRUE
GRANDMA	CR1703	FALSE
THE TELEPHONE SCAM	CR1704	TRUE
THE SLASHER UNDER THE CAR	CR1705	FALSE
THE SUPERMARKET SCAM	CR1706	FALSE
INFECTED NEEDLES	CR1707	FALSE
THE KIDNEY HEIST	CR1708	FALSE
RAZORBLADES IN WATERSLIDES	CR1709	FALSE

ANIMALS & PESTS...

SPIDERS IN PLANTS	AN1601	FALSE
THE SURREY PUMA	AN1602	UNDECIDED
COCKROACHES ON THE TONGUE	AN1603	FALSE
THE LOG FLUME HORROR	AN1604	FALSE
THE IMPORTED SNAKE	AN1605	FALSE
THE DEAD CAT PACKAGE	AN1606	FALSE
ALLIGATORS IN THE SEWERS	AN1607	UNDECIDED
KASPER, THE WOODEN CAT	AN1608	TRUE

HORROR...

THE DEAD PROFESSOR	HO4601	UNDECIDED
THE MIDNIGHT SCREAM	HO4602	FALSE
THE LICKED HAND	HO4603	FALSE
AIDS MARY	HO4604	FALSE
BURIED ALIVE!	HO4605	UNDECIDED
FLESH FOR SALE	HO4606	UNDECIDED
THE HAIRY ARMED HITCHHIKER	HO4607	UNDECIDED
THE BLAIR WITCH PROJECT	HO4608	FALSE
THE HALLOWEEN HORROR PREDICTION	HO4609	FALSE
TRICKS IN TREATS	HO4610	TRUE

TRAINS, PLANES, & AUTOMOBILES...

MOBILE PHONES AT PETROL STATIONS	TR8701	FALSE
GHOSTLY HANDPRINTS	TR8702	FALSE
THE CHICKEN GUN	TR8703	FALSE
THE ROAD HOG	TR8704	FALSE
BATTLE OF THE AGES	TR8705	FALSE
MR. GAY	TR8706	FALSE
THE LOCKED OUT PILOT	TR8707	FALSE
THE DEATH CAR	TR8708	FALSE
THE BEDBUG LETTER	TR8709	UNDECIDED
LIFE IS CHEAP	TR8710	UNDECIDED
THE JATO ROCKET CAR	TR8711	FALSE
THE CLEVER MOTORIST	TR8712	UNDECIDED
THE WOODEN AIRFIELD	TR8714	UNDECIDED

FOOD & DRINK...

KENTUCKY FRIED RAT	FD3301	FALSE
AMERICAN SOUP	FD3302	FALSE
BAR PEENUTS	FD3303	UNDECIDED
NEIMAN MARCUS COOKIES	FD3304	FALSE
DON'T SWALLOW YOUR GUM	FD3305	FALSE
COKECAINE	FD3306	TRUE
SANTA COKE	FD3307	FALSE
CARROT VISION	FD3308	TRUE

AROUND THE WORLD...

THE GUCCI KANGEROO	AW1901	FALSE
FLATJACK	AW1902	FALSE
HONEYMOON HORROR	AW1903	FALSE
FLYING COWS	AW1904	FALSE
SOUNDS LIKE ENEMY WHALES	AW1905	UNDECIDED
VOTE DONALD DUCK!	AW1906	FALSE
THE ITALIAN JOB	AW1907	UNDECIDED
THE BELGIUM BEAST	AW1908	FALSE
CLEANING UP WITH TOOTHPASTE	AW1909	FALSE
HOME IS WHERE THE AIRPORT IS	AW1910	TRUE
TWO FINGER SALUTE	AW1911	TRUE

NETLORE...

GOODTIMES	NL6501	FALSE
BUDWEISER FROGS SCREENSAVER	NL6502	FALSE
RACIST WORD	NL6503	FALSE
THE BROKEN CUP HOLDER	NL6504	TRUE
CRAIG SHERGOLD	NL6505	TRUE
INTERNET CLEAN-UP DAY	NL6506	FALSE
AIRCRAFT MAINTENANCE	NL6507	UNDECIDED
FOREIGN SIGNS	NL6508	UNDECIDED

9/11...

BERT IS EVIL	WT9801	TRUE
WINGDINGS CONSPIRACY	WT9802	FALSE
THE NOSTRADAMUS PREDICTIONS	WT9803	FALSE
THE STARBUCKS OUTRAGE	WT9804	TRUE
THE $20 PREDICTION	WT9805	TRUE
IT'S A LOTTERY	WT9806	TRUE
THE PENTAGON ATTACK	WT9807	FALSE
THE BIRMINGHAM WARNING	WT9808	FALSE
JACKIE CHAN'S LUCKY ESCAPE	WT9809	TRUE
THE COKE WARNING	WT9810	FALSE
THE DEVIL'S FACE IN THE SMOKE	WT9811	UNDECIDED

PARODIES...

BIN LADEN'S MEMO	PD7301	FALSE
THE LIVERPOOL WARNING	PD7302	FALSE
BODY PARTS	PD7303	FALSE
ULs OF ULs	PD7304	FALSE

ISBN 1-4120-4546-0